Herbert Puchta   Günter Gerngross   Peter Lewis-Jones

Super Minds

American English

Workbook 4

CAMBRIDGE
UNIVERSITY PRESS

CAMBRIDGE
UNIVERSITY PRESS

University Printing House, Cambridge CB2 8BS, United Kingdom

Cambridge University Press is part of the University of Cambridge.

It furthers the University's mission by disseminating knowledge in the pursuit of education, learning and research at the highest international levels of excellence.

www.cambridge.org
Information on this title: www.cambridge.org/9781107604339

© Cambridge University Press 2012

First published 2012
10th printing 2015

Printed in Italy by Rotolito Lombarda S.p.A.

A catalog record for this publication is available from the British Library

ISBN 978-1-107-60432-2 Student's Book with DVD-ROM 4
ISBN 978-1-107-60433-9 Workbook 4
ISBN 978-1-107-60435-3 Teacher's Book 4
ISBN 978-1-107-60436-0 Teacher's Resource Book with Audio CD 4
ISBN 978-1-107-60434-6 Class Audio CDs 4
ISBN 978-1-107-60437-7 Classware and Interactive DVD-ROM 4

Contents

Good job, Ben and Lucy!

1 **Look at the pictures and letters. Write the words.**

1 greathophopr

photographer

2 routjailns

3 pcomeiorhn

4 dabn

5 pbeurm scar

6 recrostlloare

7 reFirs lhewe

8 cruoslea

9 ymrao

2 **Read and write the words.**

1 She writes stories for newspapers.   *journalist*

2 He's the most important man in town.

3 She takes pictures.

4 They play music.

5 You speak into this.

6 Four fairground rides:

1 **Match the questions with the answers.**

1 Are you eleven?
2 What's your favorite color?
3 When do you get up in the mornings?
4 Where do you go on vacation?
5 Who is your best friend?
6 Do you like going on adventures with Ben?
7 Does Ben ever make you angry?
8 Is it fun being an Explorer?

a ☐ Yes, it is.
b ☐ Ben, of course.
c ☐ Yes, I do.
d ☐ Blue, definitely.
e ☐ Sometimes, when he's scared of silly things.
f ☐ Half past seven.
g [1] No, I'm ten.
h ☐ I go to the beach.

2 **Read and complete the questions.**

1 _How_ old are you?
2 _____ do you live?
3 _____ you have any brothers or sisters?
4 _____ your favorite color red?
5 _____ your school have a uniform?
6 _____ is your favorite subject?
7 _____ do you get home from school?
8 _____ you tell your best friend everything?

3 **Answer the questions from Activity 2 about yourself.**

1 _____
2 _____
3 _____
4 _____
5 _____
6 _____
7 _____
8 _____

1 Remember the song. Write the words in order.

fun. / Here / they / ~~The~~ / come. / and /
Adventure / and / Lucy / ~~Explorers.~~ / Ben.

The Explorers.
_____
_____
_____

stars. / Ben / are. / Here / The / and /
Action / they / Lucy. / Explorers.

_____
_____
_____
_____

2 Is it Ben or Lucy in the song? Write the sentences on the T-shirts.

I find a lot of treasure.   I like adventure.
I love exploring things.   I'm not scared of anything.

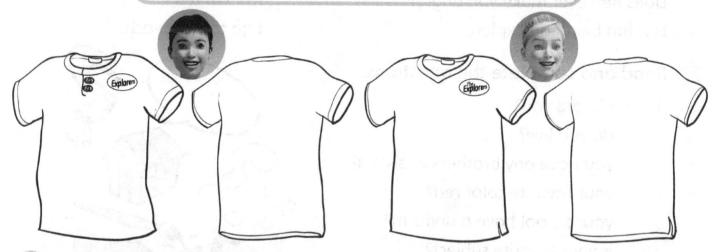

3 Answer the questions.

Are you an Explorer?

1 Do you like adventure? _____

2 Do you like exploring things? _____

3 Do you like exciting things? _____

4 Are you scared of anything? _____

Key
Q 1–3: yes = 1 point, no = 0 points
Q 4: no = 1 point, yes = 0 points

4 points: You're a true Explorer, just like Ben and Lucy.

3 points: You're almost an Explorer.

1–2 points: You aren't an Explorer yet.

0 points: You aren't really an Explorer.

CD1 10 **What did Emma do at the party? Listen and check (✓).**

2 **Read and complete the questions.**

1 What _was_ the party like?
2 _____ there a band?
3 _____ you dance?

4 _____ there a barbecue?
5 _____ you have a lot of fun?
6 _____ there bumper cars, too?

3 **Write questions for the answers.**

1 _What did you do last night_ ?

Last night? I watched TV.

2 _____ ?

I watched a movie.

3 _____ ?

Yes, it was a really good movie.

4 _____ ?

No, I didn't watch the game. I don't like soccer.

5 _____ ?

No, I didn't do my homework. I'm going to do it this weekend.

6 _____ ?

I went to bed at about ten o'clock.

1 (Think!) **Remember the story. Put the sentences in order.**

	Mr. Davidson tells them about a king.
1	The children tell Mr. Davidson about their adventure.
	Mr. Davidson shows the children a map.
	Mr. Davidson finds a symbol on the statue.
	Horax calls Zelda.
	The children see the symbol and read a rhyme on the map.

2 **Read and write the words.**

go   rhyme   quiz   is   ~~know~~   find

Study the map, so then you (1) _know_ the places where you have to (2)_____ .

When you get there, look and (3)_____ a line like this to make a (4)_____ .

The lines together make a (5)_____ to tell you where the treasure (6)_____ .

3 (Think!) **The pictures on the map tell Ben and Lucy where to look. Look, guess, and write sentences. Use words from the box.**

school   library   zoo   lake   station   ~~museum~~   concert hall
castle   statue   art gallery   restaurant   planetarium

1

I think they have to
find a museum.

2

_____

3

_____

4

_____

5

_____

6

_____

1 Match the rhyming words.

1. noise
2. rhyme
3. shoe
4. toe
5. cheese

a. trees
b. snow
c. boys
d. time
e. glue

3 Think! Which one is different in each group? Read, think, and circle.

1	bumper car	microphone	carousel	Ferris wheel
2	code	book	newspaper	treasure
3	journalist	mayor	photographer	rollercoaster
4	had	opened	wanted	used
5	famous	exciting	reading	dangerous

4 Color the bricks to make sentences. Write in the missing words.

1	_Does_ your	you go on	in a band?
2	_____ your parents	TV	yesterday?
3	Where _____	brother play	last weekend?
4	_____ you watch	you do	Spanish?
5	_____ did	speak	vacation last summer?

1 In the museum

1 Complete the words. Then draw lines.

a

b

c

d

e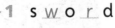

1 s w o r d
2 h __ l m __ t
3 s __ i e __ d
4 bo __ and a r r __ w
5 __ n i __ h t

6 n __ c k l a __ e
7 c r o __ n
8 b e __ t
9 q __ e e __
10 b __ a __ e l e t

f

g

h

i

j

2 Look, read, and number the sentences.

①  ② ③ ④ ⑤ ⑥

a ☐ 2 She's wearing a dress, a crown, and two bracelets.
b ☐ He's wearing a helmet. He's carrying a shield and a bow and arrow.
c ☐ He's wearing a helmet. He's carrying a shield and a sword.
d ☐ She's wearing a dress with a belt, a crown, and a bracelet.
e ☐ She's wearing a dress, a crown, a necklace, and a bracelet.
f ☐ He's carrying his helmet. He's wearing his sword on his belt.

1 Write the sentences under the pictures.

I have to drink more water.   I'm not allowed to touch my sister's CDs.
I have to take off my shoes in the house.   ~~I'm not allowed to run in the living room.~~
I have to do my homework.   I'm not allowed to eat too much ice cream.

1 I'm not allowed to run in the living room.

2 _____

3 _____

4 _____

5 _____

6 _____

2 Read and write *have to* or *'m not allowed to* and a word from the box.

shout   keep   use   wear   ~~drink~~   buy

1 I 'm not allowed to drink water from the lake. It's dirty.
2 I _____ in the house when my baby brother is sleeping.
3 I _____ a helmet when I ride my bike. It keeps my head safe.
4 I _____ the dog on his leash. I don't want him to chase cats.
5 I _____ a new T-shirt. I have too many already!
6 I _____ my camera here. The sign says "No pictures."

3 What do you have to do at home or in school? What aren't you allowed to do? Write four sentences: two with *have to* and two with *not allowed to*.

I have to wear my school uniform.

1 What does the knight say? What isn't he allowed to do in the museum? Look and write sentences.

1 I'm not allowed to _____

2 _____

3 _____

2 Remember the song. Correct the sentences.

1 The bracelets are in the vase.   The bracelets are flying around.
2 The necklaces are flying around.   _____
3 The crowns are on the ground.   _____
4 The swords are roaring.   _____
5 The vase is fighting.   _____
6 The lions are shouting.   _____

3 Describe the scene at the museum.

It's midnight at the museum. The knight is dancing. _____
_____
_____

1 Read and circle.

1 Please help <u>Bob</u>.   (him) / he

2 Please show the picture to <u>Jenna</u>.   she / her

3 Please write <u>Ruby and me</u> an email.   us / we

4 Tell the story to <u>Frank and Amy</u>.   they / them

5 Buy a new dress for <u>Mia</u>.   her / she

6 Please give the pen to <u>Jack</u>.   he / him

2 Change the sentences.

1 Don't tell Hannah.
   Don't tell her.

2 Don't show the letter to Joel
   and Frank.

3 Don't give any money to Ryan.

4 Don't take the apples!

5 Please don't shout at Bella and me.

6 Don't give any bananas to Ella.

1 **Remember the story. Read and write *t* (true) or *f* (false).**

1 Someone is trying to hurt Lucy and Ben with a shield. | *f* |
2 The knight comes after them. | |
3 The knight finds Lucy and Ben. | |
4 The knight falls down the stairs. | |
5 Lucy and Ben find a rhyme on the knight's sword. | |
6 The knight was Zelda. | |

2 **Read and write the words.**

chase   queen   children   knight   ~~dressing~~   going

Zelda,
I'm (1) _dressing_ up as the (2)_____ ! When the (3)_____
come into the museum, I'm (4)_____ to scare them. Then I'm
going to (5)_____ them. You can be the (6)_____ .
Horax

3 (Think!) **Draw lines and complete the sentences.**

1 The dinosaur _is from the Nature Museum_____ .
2 The owl_____ .
3 The motorcycle_____ .
4 The shield_____ .
5 The plane_____ .
6 The knight_____ .

1 CD1 23 **Listen and write the missing words. Then say with a friend.**

1

Tim: Look out!

Sue: What was that?

Tim: The tree. It just fell.

Sue: Wow! _____ _____ !

2

Liam: What am I going to buy you for your birthday?

Kim: _____ _____ _____ !

Liam: What?

Kim: Nothing! That's what you bought me last year!

2 **Color the squares yellow or brown.**

yellow	brown	bow and arrow	crown
know	window	how	town
show	now	flower	snow

3 CD1 24 **Listen, say, and check your answers.**

1 **Values** **What can we learn from the story? Color the words.**

Knowing   Talking   a lot   can't   can

find   help   you   I   in   out

your   their   life   name   .

2 **Read and write the words.**

case   daughter   flashlight   checked   ~~interesting~~   locked   piece   key

1   Mr. Benson told children ___interesting___ stories.

2   The best _____ in the museum was a statue of a gold cat.

3   The statue was in a glass _____ .

4   When Mr. Benson went home, he always _____ the windows and the doors.

5   He had an 18-year-old _____ named Cleo.

6   After the party, Mr. Benson took the _____ to the museum and closed the window.

7   He _____ the alarm.

8   When Cleo heard a noise, she waited, and then she turned on her _____ .

3 **Think!** **Draw the missing symbol in Box 3.**

Listen and draw a line from the day to the correct picture.

Monday

Tuesday

Wednesday

History

Thursday

Friday

Saturday

Sunday

1 **Read and write the words.**

> collection   exhibits   galleries   ~~ancient~~

1 very old _ancient_

2 objects in a museum _____

3 a group of objects that are the same _____

4 rooms in a museum _____

2 (Values) **Read the story. What can we learn from it? Check (✓).**

My grandpa likes to tell me stories about when he was young. We live in the city, but when my grandpa was a boy, he lived on a farm high up in the mountains.

When we go shopping, we get into the car and drive to the supermarket. We do the shopping, put it in the car, and drive home.

When my grandpa went shopping, he walked down the mountain, then he bought things in a small store in a small town, he put them in his backpack, and then he walked back to the farm again. He didn't buy very much, just the things that they didn't have at the farm, such as flour, oil, and salt.

On the farm they baked their own bread. One day my grandpa took me to a museum. There they showed us how to bake bread. My grandpa said, "That's how we baked our bread on the farm." We tasted the bread in the museum, and it was really good.

Last winter I went skiing with my family, and we stayed in a hut in the mountains. For the first few days, there was a lot of sun and we skied, but then it snowed for three days. It was too dangerous to leave the hut, and soon we had no more bread. Then I remembered my grandpa. "I can bake bread," I said to my parents, but they didn't believe me.

We had water, oil, and salt, and luckily we found some flour in a cabinet. I remembered what my grandpa told me and baked some bread. It wasn't really very good, but everybody liked it because they were hungry.

- [ ] We cannot learn anything from history.
- [ ] We can never do the same things that people did a long time ago.
- [ ] We can learn a lot from history.

1 **CD 1 27** (Think!) Archeologists found these objects. What did people use them for? Listen and number the pictures.

a  b  c  d 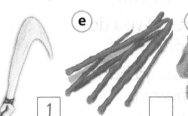 e 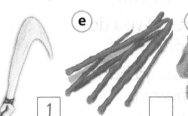 f

a ☐ b ☐ c ☐ d [1] e ☐ f ☐

2 **Look, read, and write the words.**

> big   didn't   fruit   gardening   Germany   loved   know   ~~tried~~

1

Giant Shoe Museum, Washington, U.S.A.

2

British Lawnmower Museum, Merseyside, U.K.

3

Banana Museum, Washington, U.S.A.

4

German Sausage Museum, Thuringia, Germany

1 I _tried_____ a pair, but they were too _____ for me.

2 Dad loves _____ , so we went to this museum, but I _____ like it.

3 There was everything that you want to _____ about this _____ !

4 My brother _____ this museum in _____ . He loves meat.

1 **Match the questions with the answers.**

1 When did you leave the museum?

2 What did you do outside?

3 Did you go back in the morning?

4 So what did you do?

5 Did you like it outside?

6 Are you going to go out again?

a ☐ No, I didn't. The window was closed.

b ☐ I don't think so. Mr. Benson said, "I will not forget to close the windows."

c ☐ 1 Three nights ago when Mr. Benson forgot to close a window.

d ☐ I met another cat, and we hunted rats.

e ☐ Yes, it was great.

f ☐ I waited, and the next night someone opened the window.

2 **Look at Activity 1. Underline the mistakes. Then write the correct sentences.**

One night Mr. Benson <u>left a door open</u>. The Egyptian cat got out of its glass case.

Outside, it met a dog. When the Egyptian cat wanted to get back in, the door was locked. She waited, and two nights later someone opened a window. She went back into her glass case.

One night Mr. Benson left a window open.

3 **Imagine that a different exhibit escaped. Write what happened.**

- Which exhibit escaped?
- What did it do outside?
- When did it go back to the museum?

One day Mr. Benson left the window open again. The ...

1 Write the words in three groups.

> ~~ancient~~ ~~belt~~ ~~bow and arrow~~ bracelet collection crown
> exhibits galleries helmet necklace shield sword

1
ancient

2
belt

3
bow and arrow

2 Look at Activity 1. Number the topics to match the groups.

☐ For fighting   ☐ Museum words   ☐ For wearing

3 Look and draw lines to make sentences.

1 Give

us	the	balls	yesterday, please.
them	a	shoes	tomorrow, please.
me	an	ball	now, please.

2 I

should	make	silence	in the museum.
'm not allowed to	be	pictures	in the store.
have to	take	a noise	in the zoo.

3 You

have to	brush	your hair	before bed.
can't	wash	your face	after bed.
should	dry	your teeth	in bed.

4 The dog

is	hungry.	Give me	some water, please.
am	thirsty.	Give them	any more, please.
are	tired.	Give him	no more, please.

1 Find and write eight words. Look →, ↓, and ↘.

1 _field_

3 _____

m	f	r	i	p	l	a	k	r	u
o	p	s	f	s	a	p	g	i	z
u	e	f	i	t	n	t	j	v	f
n	b	o	e	l	d	e	h	e	o
t	s	i	l	l	a	r	e	r	r
a	r	i	d	f	o	k	p	a	e
i	s	l	a	n	d	s	e	f	s
n	a	t	o	w	n	v	e	r	t

2 _____

4 _____

5 _____

6 _____

7 _____

8 _____

2 Read and write words from Activity 1.

1 **A:** Can we swim to that _island_ in the middle of the lake?

  B: No, you can't, but look, we can all go on that boat.

2 **A:** I can see some lights there. What is that?

  B: There are a few houses. It's a small _____ .

3 **A:** Let's go through the trees.

  B: No, I think we should stay on the _____ . It's safer.

4 **A:** How can we get across the _____ ?

  B: Look, there's a bridge.

5 **A:** Why can't we go into that _____ ?

  B: Because they're cutting down some trees. It's too dangerous.

1 Find and write four sentences.

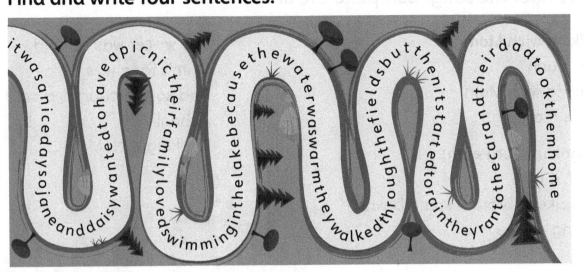

1   It was a nice day, so Jane and Daisy wanted to have a picnic.

2   _____

3   _____

4   _____

2 Join the sentences with *and*, *but*, *so*, and *because*.

1   There are fields close to our town. People love having picnics there.

    There are fields close to our town, and people love having picnics there.

2   It started to rain. We went home.

    _____

3   John went to the U.S.A. He stayed in Chicago.

    _____

4   Kate liked visiting her uncle. It took two hours by car.

    _____

5   The movie was boring. We left the movie theater.

    _____

6   Don't go across that old bridge. It's dangerous.

    _____

3 Write four sentences about you. Use *and*, *but*, *so*, and *because*.

I like watching soccer, and …	I like watching soccer, but …

1 **Remember the song. Complete the lines.**

Walking with Mom
Is so much ⁽¹⁾ _fun_ .
Walking with Mom
In the morning ⁽²⁾ _____ .

We got up very early.
What a nice ⁽³⁾ _____ !
We walked through some towns,
Singing all the ⁽⁴⁾ _____ .

"Let's sit here," said Mom
And pointed to some ⁽⁵⁾ _____ .
"We can have a picnic –
I have some bread and ⁽⁶⁾ _____ ."
Walking with Mom ...

We walked through the fields,
But that was a ⁽⁷⁾ _____ .
Mom didn't see the path
And fell into the ⁽⁸⁾ _____ !

The water was so cold,
Mom's face was ⁽⁹⁾ _____
And so she caught a cold.
Achoo! ⁽¹⁰⁾ _____ !
Walking with Mom ...

2 **Complete Mom's email to her friend Sally.**

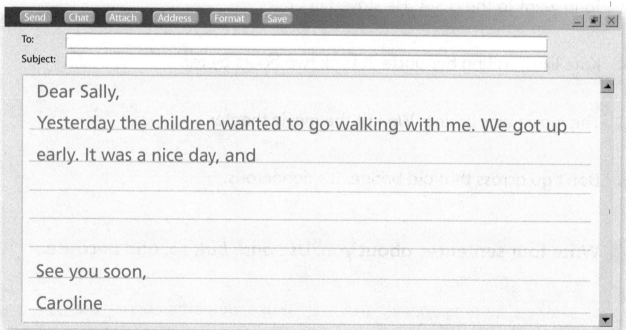

Send Chat Attach Address Format Save

To:
Subject:

Dear Sally,

Yesterday the children wanted to go walking with me. We got up

early. It was a nice day, and

See you soon,

Caroline

1 Look at Superman and Superwoman's photo album. What could they do 40 years ago? Write sentences. Use the words from the box.

> lift up (x 2)   ~~fight with~~   run faster than (x 2)   ride on   jump from   climb

1   40 years ago, Superman could fight with a crocodile.

2   _____

3   _____

4   _____

5   _____

6   _____

7   _____

8   _____

2 What can you do now that you couldn't do when you were younger? Write sentences.

When I was three, I couldn't read and write. _____

_____

_____

1 **Remember the story. Read and write the words.**

> saw   was   helped   pocket   hungry
> town   missing   ~~walk~~   waiter   menu

Ben and Lucy went for a great (1) _walk_ with Ben's grandpa. When they felt (2) _____ , Grandpa took them to a nice restaurant in a little (3) _____ . Buster (4) _____ hungry, too. At the restaurant Grandpa (5) _____ that Ben and Lucy had a map. Ben and Lucy wanted to tell Ben's grandpa about it, but the (6) _____ came and brought the soup, so Ben put the map in his (7) _____ . Later, Ben found out that the map was (8) _____ . Grandpa said, "I didn't like the waiter very much, so I put a (9) _____ in your pocket and kept the map." Then Grandpa (10) _____ the children find the symbol and the line of the rhyme.

2 Think! **Make words with the letters of _restaurant_.**

aunt, run, _____

_____

3 Think! **Complete the waiter's diary entry.**

Today there was an (1) _old man_ in the restaurant. He was with two (2) _____ . They (3) _____ for lunch. When I took the soup, I saw (4) _____ on the table. I wanted to know about it, so I took (5) _____ to their table. One child said the next picture on the map was (6) _____ , but the other one said that you don't find (7) _____ . I took the map with me, but when I looked at it in the kitchen, I saw that it (8) _____ . I think the old man took the map and put the menu (9) _____ . I was very (10) _____ !

1 CD1 38 **Listen and write the missing words. Then say with a friend.**

1

Jen: Mr. Price, this is for your new house.

Mr. Price: _____ _____

_____ plant! Thank you! That's very kind.

2

Dawn: Did you see those two men in the car?

Dan: Yes. What about them?

Dawn: _____ _____

_____ _____

_____ them.

Dan: What do you mean?

Dawn: One had a T-shirt and shorts, and the other had a big winter coat and boots!

2 **Make sentences. Then circle the silent consonants.**

1 The knight   a ☐ knows about volcanoes.

2 Please write   b ☐ thing to do.

3 The scientist   c 1 has a sword.

4 The rhinos live   d ☐ listen to the teacher.

5 That's the wrong   e ☐ a rhyme in your notebooks.

6 In school you have to   f ☐ on an island.

3 CD1 39 **Listen, say, and check your answers.**

1 CD 1 40 **Listen and write _t_ (true) or _f_ (false).**

1 For her birthday party, Kate invited three friends. — f

2 One of her presents was a book about butterflies. — ☐

3 Kate's favorite present was her new pencil case. — ☐

4 At half past nine, Dad took the children for a night walk. — ☐

5 The wind in the trees sounded like animals. — ☐

6 Kate's uncle and dad played a trick on her. — ☐

2 **Write the story. Use the pictures and the sentences from Activity 1 to help you.**

It was Kate's birthday. She invited her friend Lisa to the party.

3 (Values) **What can we learn from the story? Check (✓).**

☐ Spending money on presents is important.

☐ Spending time with your friends and family is important.

☐ Having a party is important.

1 Look and read. Write 1, 2, or 3 words to complete the sentences about the story.

Hide and sleep

Last week Mom and Dad took us to the furniture store. They wanted to buy a new couch because our old one wasn't very comfortable. My brother and I weren't very happy because we don't really like shopping, but then Mom said that Grandpa wanted to come, too. We liked that idea because Grandpa is cool!

The store was really big. Mom and Dad left us with Grandpa and went to look at furniture. Grandpa had a great idea. "This store is very big," he said, "so let's have a game of hide and seek." We were really excited because there were so many places to hide. My brother hid first, and after ten minutes I found him

behind a cabinet. Then it was my turn, but Grandpa found me very quickly. Finally it was Grandpa's turn. We closed our eyes and counted to 100. "Coming!" we shouted. We looked and we looked, but we couldn't find Grandpa anywhere. After half an hour, Mom and Dad came back. "Where's Grandpa?" they asked. Now the entire family started to look for him. When we were in the part of the store where they had beds, we heard a funny noise. "Shhh!" said Dad. "Someone is snoring." We looked across the store and there on the most comfortable bed was Grandpa – asleep!

1 The family went shopping for _a new couch_ .
2 The children really like their _____ .
3 Grandpa wanted to play _____ .
4 It took them _____ to find the first person.
5 _____ the last person to hide.
6 After _____ minutes, their parents came back.
7 The family heard _____ .
8 They found Grandpa in the store, sleeping on the _____ .

1 **Look at the paintings. Write five sentences. Use the words from the box or your own ideas.**

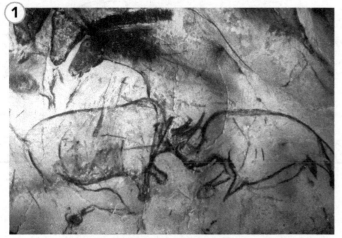

most beautiful   most modern   oldest
most difficult to understand   most interesting

I think painting number two is the …

I like number four best because …

I don't like number one, but … because …

Think! **Read Danny's text and think. Which picture is he describing?**

> I think this is a beautiful picture, and it's very interesting. It isn't easy to understand at first. When I look at it for a long time, this is what I imagine: there's a river with a big waterfall, and there's a fish in the lake at the bottom. The water is very fast.

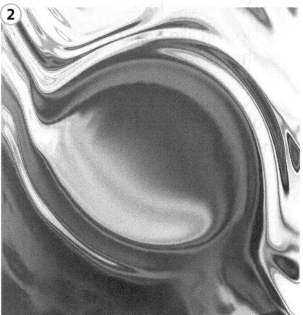

Picture ☐

  Look and imagine. What do you see? Write about the other picture from Activity 1.

_____

_____

_____

_____

1 Match the questions with the answers.

1 What do you prefer doing in your free time, Isabel?

2 What activities do you like doing outdoors?

3 And what do you like doing at home?

4 Do you spend a lot of time on the Internet?

5 What about being in town? Do you like that?

6 Do you like going shopping?

a ☐ I love walking, watching birds, and helping in the garden.

b ☐ Not very much because there are too many cars and it's noisy.

c ☐ Yes, I use it every day to look for information, and I write emails.

d ☐ I love reading a lot. When I have a good book, I can't stop. I never watch TV.

e ☐ Yes, I do. Sometimes I go with Mom, and we have lots of fun.

f ☐ 1 When the weather is nice, I prefer being outdoors. When it rains, I love staying home.

2 Look at Activity 1. <u>Underline</u> the mistakes. Then write the correct sentences.

Isabel is very much an outdoor person. She <u>likes riding her bike</u>. She also likes listening to birds and sleeping in the garden. When the weather is nice, she loves being at home. She watches a lot of TV. She never uses a computer, so she doesn't send emails. Isabel doesn't like being in town very much. She thinks that there are too many people.

She loves walking.

_____

_____

_____

3 Write about your free time.

I'm an outdoor person.

1 (Think!) **Which one is different in each group? Look, think, and circle.**

①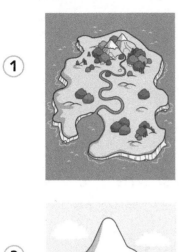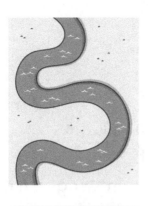

②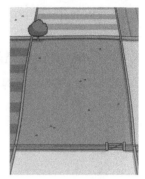

③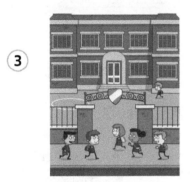

2 **Color the bricks to make sentences. Write in the missing words.**

1	He liked the book,	was young,	they saw a snake.
2	They were scared	and	write.
3	When Grandma	two, I _____	she _____ run really fast.
4	When I was	_____	went to bed.
5	She was tired,	_____ she	he _couldn't_ stop reading it!

③ Danger!

① Complete the words.

1 f i r e
2 _ m b _ l _ n c _
3 f l _ _ d
4 p _ l _ c _ c _ r
5 p _ r _ m _ d _ c

6 f _ r _ f _ g h t _ r
7 p _ l _ c _ _ _ f f _ c _ r
8 f _ r _ _ n g _ n _
9 _ m _ r g _ n c y s _ r v _ c _ s

② Complete the diagram with the words from Activity 1.

```
People                    Emergency              Dangers
_____          services               fire _____
_____                                 _____

                          Vehicles
          _____          _____
```

③ Read and complete the text. Use the words from Activity 2.

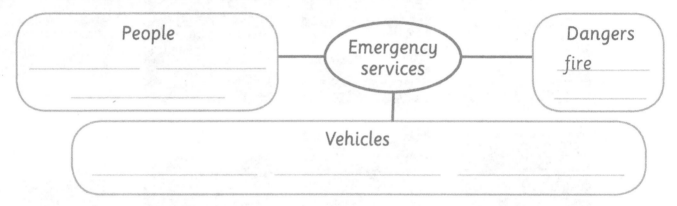

One day I was on my way to school, and I saw smoke. It was coming out of a house. I had my cell phone, so I called the (1) _emergency services_ . Five minutes later, a big red (2) _____ came down the road. It stopped and four (3) _____ got out. It was really exciting. They started to fight the (4) _____ , and there was water everywhere! It was like a (5) _____ . Then an (6) _____ arrived with two (7) _____ , but there wasn't anyone in the house, so they went back to the hospital. Finally two (8) _____ arrived. "Do you live here?" one of them asked me. "No, I don't," I said, "but I called 911." "That's good," the other one said, "but you should be at school now. What school do you go to?" "Castle Park," I answered. "OK, we can take you," one of them said ... and I got a ride in a (9) _____ !

1 **Write *was* or *were*.**

Yesterday at 11 o'clock in the park,

1   … Tim _was_ riding his bike,

2   … Mr. Brown _____ reading a newspaper,

3   … Ian and Ruth _____ playing soccer,

4   … my dog _____ chasing a ball,

5   … Sara _____ running,

6   … and Mr. and Mrs. Smith _____ walking their dog.

2 **Describe the picture. Use the words from the box.**

talk   fight   try   sing   ~~watch~~

Yesterday at eight o'clock,

1   … Mom and Dad _were watching TV_ _____,

2   … my brother _____,

3   … my sister _____,

4   … the dog and the cat _____,

5   … and I _____ to do my homework!

1 **Remember the song. Look and number the objects.**

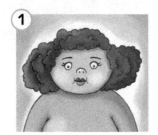
1

2

3

4

5

a ☐
b ☐
c ☐
d ☐
e 1

2 **Complete the sentences.**

1 Dad _was fixing the lights_____ .

2 Emily was _____ .

3 Jonathan was _____ .

4 I was _____ .

5 Mom was _____ .

3 **Think!** **What were these people doing? Imagine and write sentences.**

1 Grandma _____ .

2 Aunt Vicky _____ .

3 Cousin Bob _____ .

4 The baby _____ .

1 **Match the questions with the answers.**

1 What was Jack doing at seven o'clock? a ☐ I was doing my homework.
2 What were you and Sue doing? b 1 He was playing computer games.
3 What was the cat doing? c ☐ They were playing cards.
4 What was Jill doing at eight o'clock? d ☐ It was sleeping.
5 What were you doing? e ☐ We were watching TV.
6 What were Bill and Liz doing? f ☐ She was listening to music.

2 **Look and write questions for the answers.**

1	2	3	4
Grandma	Grandpa	Nathan and Jacob	Dad

1 What _was Grandma doing at three o'clock_ ?
She was gardening.

2 _____, Grandpa?
I was reading a book.

3 _____ ?
They were riding their bikes.

4 _____ ?
He was cooking.

3 **Read the questions and answers. Answer the questions about yourself.**

What was Bea's family doing ...	Her little brother and sister ...	You
... at six o'clock?	... were sleeping.	I was sleeping.
... at seven o'clock?	... were playing.	
... at eight o'clock?	... were having breakfast.	
... at nine o'clock?	... were having a swimming lesson with Mom.	
... at ten o'clock?	... were arriving at the store.	

1 **Think!** **Remember the story. Read and circle.**

1 Why does Ben's grandpa say, "Stay in the car, please?"
   A Because he wants Lucy to talk to the operator.
   B Because it's too dangerous for them.

2 Why does the operator ask Lucy about the house number?
   A Because she wants to know where Lucy lives.
   B Because she's going to send an ambulance and a fire engine there.

3 Why does Ben's grandpa say to the man, "Quick! We have to get you out."?
   A Because the man's leg hurts.
   B Because it's dangerous to stay in the car after the accident.

4 Why does Ben's grandpa say, "Don't go so fast."?
   A Because the man on the motorcycle is a dangerous driver.
   B Because the man on the motorcycle is making them wet.

2 **Think!** **How useful are these people? Write 2, 1, or 0.**

> 2 points = very useful   1 point = useful   0 points = not useful at all

a | 0

Help! It's terrible! Please help! Come here!

b

Hello. This is John Brown. I'm on Station Road across from the supermarket. There's an accident. There's a man. He can't walk.

c

Hi, this is Betty Miller. I'm on West Street. There's a car on fire and … it looks dangerous.

d

Wow! An accident, look! Climb up here and you can see it better!

1 CD 2 12 **Listen and write the missing words. Then say with a friend.**

1

Zak: Where are you going?

Alien: Back to my planet.

Zak: _____

_____

_____ ?

Alien: Of course you can.

Zak: Great, but I need to be back for dinner at six o'clock.

2

SMASH!

May: There was an accident outside our house last night! We were watching TV, and _____

_____

loud noise. I ran to the window and saw two cars.

Liam: Did you call the police?

May: No, I didn't because I could see that no one was hurt ... and one of them was a police car!

2 **Complete the words.**

1   kn*ight*_____

2   wh_____

3   l_____ning

4   midn_____

5   firef_____er

6   k_____

3 CD 2 13 **Listen, say, and check your answers.**

1 (Values) **What can we learn from the story? Color the words.**

Quick   Slow   listening   thinking

can   help   escape

save   people   water   .

2 **Answer the questions. Use your imagination.**

Imagine it is December 24, 2004. Think about these questions:

- Where is Tilly?
- What is the weather like?
- What is she doing?

Now use your answers to complete Tilly's postcard.

Dear Rachel,
I'm having a fantastic time here in

_____

_____

I can't wait for Christmas tomorrow!
Lots of love,
Tilly

3 **Write another postcard from Tilly on December 28, 2004.**

Tilly tells Rachel:

- where she is
- what happened
- what she did
- what she is going to do now

1 Look and read. Choose the correct words and write them on the lines.

a hut

a hotel

a snorkel

a sandcastle

1 This is a building.
   You stay here when
   you are on vacation.   _a hotel_

2 This is very cold.
   You eat it, and
   it tastes sweet.   _____

3 You can breathe
   under water with this.   _____

4 This is a very big wave.
   It is very dangerous.   _____

5 This is a small building.
   Some are houses. Some
   are stores.   _____

6 Children like to build
   this on the beach.   _____

7 This is a person
   who is on vacation.   _____

a tourist

a beach ball

a tsunami

an ice cream cone

2 Find six differences. Write sentences.

A

B

In picture A the sandcastle is …

1 Values Read the story. What can we learn from it? Check (✓).

1

Tara: What's that funny smell?
Matt: Oh, no … the house is on fire.
Follow me and do exactly what I say.

2

Tara: I have to get my teddy bear!
Matt: Where is he?
Tara: Upstairs, of course. In my bedroom.
Matt: I'm sorry – it's too dangerous.

3

Tara: I can't breathe with all this smoke.
Matt: Don't worry. Get down on your knees
like this and crawl.

4

Matt: There isn't as much smoke here.
Tara: Can I stand up?
Matt: Yes, but let me close the door to stop
the fire. Let's get to the back door.

5

Tara: Are we safe now?
Matt: Yes, we are, but let's get away from
the house. I'm going to call the emergency
services.

6

Firefighter: Good job! Your actions saved
your lives and most of your house.
Matt: Thanks. It was something that they
taught us at school.
Tara: Teddy! You're alive!

☐ When there's a fire, take pictures of it.

☐ When you smell smoke, open the window.

☐ Knowing what to do in a fire can save lives.

1 **Read and draw the escape routes.**

From my bedroom: go downstairs and out of the front door.
If the fire is on the stairs, go to my parents' room and climb
onto the kitchen roof.

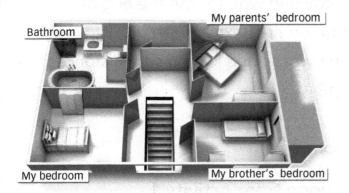

2 **Think!** **Draw escape plans for your house.**

3 **Write escape plans from:**

- your bedroom
- the kitchen
- the living room

1 CD2 15 **Put the dialog in order. Then listen and check.**

☐ **B:** When is it going to arrive?

☐ **A:** Good, so you're safe. Is there anyone in number 37?

☐ **B:** I'm calling from 39 Grange Road. The fire's at number 37.

1 **A:** Hello. How can we help you?

☐ **B:** Yes, I am.

☐ **A:** OK. Don't go in to check. Stay and wait for the fire engine.

☐ **B:** I'm calling to report a house on fire next door to us.

☐ **A:** In about five minutes. Don't worry, and keep a safe distance.

☐ **A:** Where are you calling from?

☐ **B:** I'm not sure.

☐ **A:** And are you outside the house?

2 **Look and write a dialog. Use language from Activity 1.**

Hello, how can we help you?

_____

_____

_____

_____

_____

_____

_____

1 **Write the words in four groups.**

accident   ambulance   banana cupcake   fire   fire engine   flood
hut   ice cream   police car   sandcastle   snorkel   vanilla shake

1
accident

2
ambulance

3
banana cupcake

4
hut

2 **Look at Activity 1. Number the topics to match the groups.**

☐ Dangers   ☐ Emergency services

☐ On the beach   ☐ Food words

3 **Look and draw lines to make sentences.**

1 We

was	playing	cards	at two o'clock yesterday.
are	watching	TV	at five o'clock yesterday.
were	making	with toys	at seven o'clock yesterday.

2 What

was	you	did	in here this morning?
is	your	do	in here tomorrow?
were	yours	doing	in here next Tuesday?

3 Was

she	flying	the piano	at eight o'clock?
they	doing	a kite	at nine o'clock?
he	playing	his homework	at ten o'clock?

4 I

was	watch	TV on	three o'clock.
were	watched	TV at	four o'clock.
is	watching	TV in	five o'clock.

4 Two round-trip tickets

1 Match and write the words.

plat	driver
ticket	of tea
train	lator
esca	case
a cup of	airs
a cup	form
back	tion
st	coffee
suit	pack
sta	office

2 platform

1 _____

3 _____

5 _____

4 _____

6 _____

7 _____ 8 _____ 9 _____ 10 _____

2 Read and write the words.

1 This is a popular drink. You make it from beans. _coffee_____

2 Trains leave from and arrive at it. _____

3 You carry your things in it. You carry it on your back. _____

4 You walk up or down them. _____

5 You carry your things in it. You move it with your hand. _____

6 It takes you up or down. _____

7 You buy your ticket here. _____

8 You wait here for the train to arrive. _____

1 Read and circle.

1 The train leaves **at** / **on** six.

2 Dinner is **on** / **at** eight.

3 I'm going to ride my bike **in** / **on** the afternoon.

4 The volleyball game is **at** / **on** Saturday.

5 It was very hot **in** / **on** April.

6 We sometimes watch TV **at** / **in** the evening.

2 Write at, in, or on.

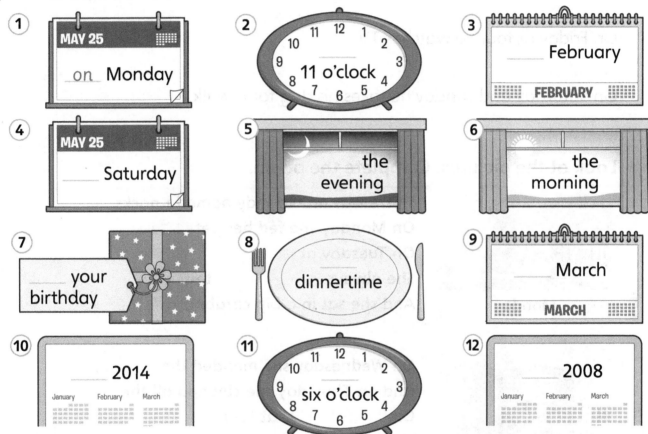

1 _on_ Monday

2 ___ 11 o'clock

3 ___ February FEBRUARY

4 ___ Saturday MAY 25

5 ___ the evening

6 ___ the morning

7 ___ your birthday

8 ___ dinnertime

9 ___ March MARCH

10 ___ 2014 January February March

11 ___ six o'clock

12 ___ 2008 January February March

3 Write sentences about yourself.

When do you …

1 … do your homework?

  I do my homework in the evening.

2 … watch TV?

3 … go to bed?

4 … have lunch?

5 … relax?

6 What month is your birthday?

1 Remember the song. Correct the sentences.

1 On Monday at five he sails his big canoe.

   On Monday at three he climbs the apple tree.

2 On Tuesday at three he plays soccer.

_____

3 On Wednesday at six he plays sports in the sports center.

_____

4 On Thursday at two he flies his kite.

_____

5 On Friday at four he watches TV.

_____

6 On Saturday and Sunday he takes his dog for a walk.

_____

2 Look at the pictures. Complete the poem.

Monday

There was an old lady named Knocks.
On Monday she fed her pet (1) *fox* .
On Tuesday at (2)_____
She always (3)_____ **tea**
And she sat in a big cardboard (4)_____ .

Tuesday

On Wednesday she mended the (5)_____
And on Thursday she cleaned all the (6)_____ .
On (7)_____ **at four**
She painted the (8)_____ .
That funny, old lady named Knocks!

Wednesday

Thursday

Friday

3 CD2 22 Listen and check. Say the poem.

1 **Write *was* or *were*.**

When the train arrived, …

1 … I <u>was</u> eating a sandwich,

2 … John and Peter _____ waiting on the platform,

3 … a man _____ reading a newspaper,

4 … two men _____ talking,

5 … a girl _____ sitting on her suitcase,

6 … and a boy _____ buying a ticket.

2 **Write sentences. Use the words from the box.**

> sit / yard   build / tree house   ride / bike   ~~play / volleyball~~

When it started to rain, …

1 … <u>they were playing volleyball.</u>

2 … _____ .

3 … _____ .

4 … _____ .

3 **Write the verbs to complete the sentences.**

1 Dad <u>was working</u> in the yard when he <u>hurt</u> his leg. (work / hurt)

2 I _____ my homework when you _____ me. (do / call)

3 When I _____ the party, my friends _____ . (leave / dance)

4 I _____ to music when Mom _____ me. (listen / call)

1 **Remember the story. Complete the sentences.**

1 At Broom station, Lucy and Ben _see Horax and Zelda_ .

2 Ben tells Lucy to _____ .

3 Zelda and Horax want to _____ .

4 Ben can see that the train is _____ .

5 When the conductor comes, Horax can't _____ .

6 Horax and Zelda have to _____ .

2 **Write sentences. Use the words from the box.**

Lucy's ~~Ben's~~ Horax's Ben and Lucy's Horax and Zelda's

1
2
3
4
5

1 _This is Ben's dog._

2 _____

3 _____

4 _____

5 _____

3 **What happened in the tunnel? Complete the story.**
Use the verbs from the box and other words.

put stood took ~~went~~

When they _went_ through _____ , Ben _____ up.

He _____ out of _____ ,

and he _____ .

1 CD2 26 Listen and write the missing words. Then say with a friend.

Anna: When are we going to wrap Dad's present?

James: Well, he's working in the yard right now, look.

Anna: Great! _____

_____ !

Hannah: Hey, Joe. What's that?

Joe: What? Where?

Hannah: That. Can't you see?

_____ _____

_____ .

Joe: I can't see anything.

Hannah: Oh, it isn't there now.

Joe: Hey! My chips!

2 Look, read, and write the words.

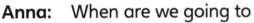

chair   pear   stairs   wearing   hair   ~~bears~~

1 He's **scared** of the _bears_ .

2 **Claire** has long _____ .

3 Please **share** the _____ .

4 **Where** are the _____ ?

5 He's _____ an old **pair** of pants.

6 It's over **there** on that _____ .

3 CD2 27 Listen, say, and check your answers.

1 CD2 28 Listen and check (✓) the box.

1 Who was on the platform?

A ✓ B ☐ C ☐

2 Who was on the train?

A ☐ B ☐ C ☐

3 What happened after the tunnel?

A ☐ B ☐ C ☐

4 What happened at the station?

A ☐ B ☐ C ☐

5 What did the old lady do?

A ☐ B ☐ C ☐

1 Read and write the correct prices.

1	London	$7.80
2	Cambridge	
3	Oxford	
4	Bristol	
5	Newcastle	
6	Hull	

1 A: How much is a one-way ticket to London?
B: It's seven dollars and eighty cents.
A: Here you go.
B: Thanks, and there's your change.

2 A: How much is a one-way ticket to Cambridge?
B: That's five dollars and twenty.
A: Here you go.
B: Thanks. Here's your ticket.

3 A: A ticket to Oxford, please. How much is it?
B: One way or round trip?
A: One way.
B: It's seven dollars and sixty cents.
A: Here you go.

4 A: How much is a one-way ticket to Bristol?
B: It's twelve forty.
A: Twelve fifty?
B: No, it's twelve dollars and forty cents.

5 A: One way to Newcastle, please. How much is it?
B: Twenty-six dollars.
A: Here you go.
B: Thank you. Here's your change.

6 A: How much is a ticket to Hull?
B: One way or round trip?
A: One way.
B: It's nineteen dollars and seventy cents.

2 Write sentences with *o'clock, half past,* or *a quarter to/past.*

Cambridge

The train to
Cambridge leaves
at twelve o'clock.

Oxford

_____
_____
_____

Newcastle

_____
_____
_____

Bristol

_____
_____
_____

London

_____
_____
_____

Hull

_____
_____
_____

1 **Look and write the words.**

push ~~fall~~ drop smooth pull rough

1 fall _____ 2 _____ 3 _____

4 _____ 5 _____ 6 _____

2 (Values) **Read and check (✓) the correct picture.**

When you lift a heavy box, you should always push up from the bottom. Don't pull the box up because it hurts your back.

1a ☐   1b ☐

Be careful when something is too high for you. Put a stepladder close to the shelf. Stand on the stepladder and put your arms out, but keep your body straight. Don't lean away from the stepladder.

2a ☐   2b ☐

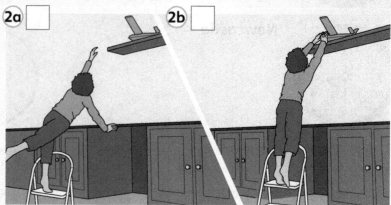

1 **Read and write the words.**

rough   stop   faster   smooth   ~~go down~~

1   When you _go down_ a slide, gravity pulls you to the bottom.

2   There is also a force trying to _____ you. It is called friction.

3   If the surface of the slide is _____ , the friction is bigger.
    You go more slowly.

4   If the surface of the slide is _____ , the friction is smaller.
    You go _____ .

2 **Think!** **Read and write 1, 2, or 3.**

These children are going at the same speed on their bikes. Then they put on their brakes. Look at the surface where they are riding. Which bike is going to stop first? Number the pictures 1 (the first) to 3 (the last).

a

b

c

1 CD2 30 **Put the dialog in order. Then listen and check.**

	A:	To London. OK. When do you want to leave?
	B:	Here you go.
	A:	One way or round trip?
	B:	Half past eight is fine. How much is the ticket?
1	A:	Hello. How can I help you?
	B:	Thank you. Oh, and what platform number is it, please?
	A:	The round-trip ticket is $42.
	B:	Round trip, please.
	A:	Thanks. And here's your change.
	B:	I want to go to London, please.
	A:	Platform 2.
	B:	In the morning.
	A:	There's a train at seven and one at half past eight.

2 **Look and write a dialog. Use language from Activity 1.**

Hello. Can I help you?

_____

_____

_____

_____

_____

_____

_____

_____

_____

_____

_____

_____

_____

1 Think! Which one is different in each group? Look, think, and circle.

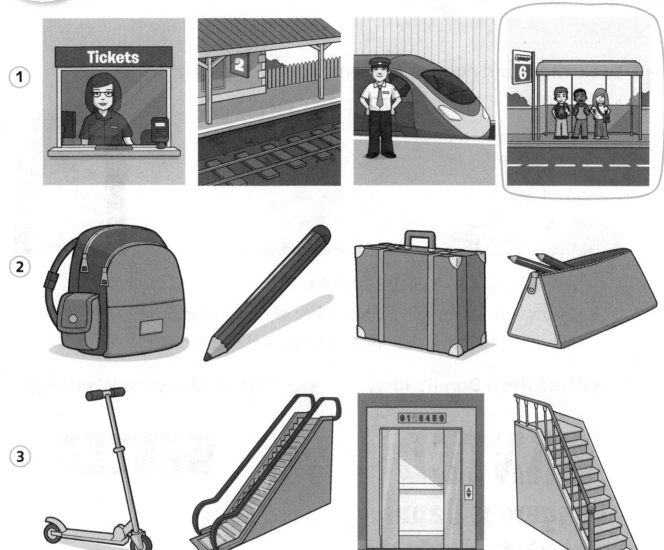

2 Color the bricks to make sentences. Write in the missing words.

1	When the train	_____ TV when	Saturday.
2	My birthday party	arrived, Dad was	you called me.
3	I was	vacation _____	August for two weeks.
4	We're going on	too fast	when he _____ an accident.
5	Paul was driving	is _____	buying a _cup_ of coffee.

5 Police!

1 **Look, read, and number the sentences.**

①  ②  ③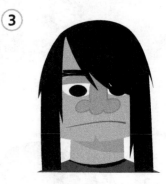

a ☐ He has long, dark hair. It's straight.

b ☐ He has light, curly hair. He has a beard and a mustache.

c ☐ He has short, blond hair. He has a scar below his mouth.

2 **Read and draw Danni's face.**

3 **Write and draw a *Wanted* poster.**

WANTED
Dangerous Danni

She has long hair. It's black. She has a long scar on her face and a small scar between her eyes. She's very dangerous.

DON'T speak to her. Call the police!

WANTED

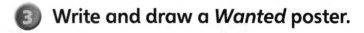

1 Look at the pictures. Read and write *t* (true) or *f* (false).

1980 Now

1 Dad used to have long hair. `t`
2 Dad used to have a scar. ☐
3 Dad used to have a beard. ☐
4 Dad used to have a mustache. ☐
5 Dad used to have straight hair. ☐
6 Dad used to have dark hair. ☐

2 Complete the sentences. Use the words from the box.

cry   sleep   eat   ~~drink~~   play   crawl

When I was a baby, …

1 I _used to drink_ milk.

2 I _____ a lot.

3 I _____ in a crib.

4 I _____ baby food.

5 I _____ on my hands and knees.

6 I _____ with my teddy bear.

3 Write sentences about you.

When I was four, …

1 _____

2 _____

3 _____

1 Remember the song. What did Dad use to look like?
Check (✓) the correct pictures.

1 a  ☐   b  ☐   c  ☐

2 a 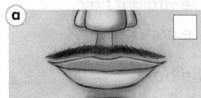 ☐   b  ☐   c 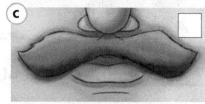 ☐

3 a  ☐   b 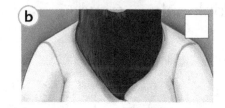 ☐   c  ☐

2 Write four sentences about Mom.

Mom used to wear glasses.

_____

_____

_____

Mom before   **Mom now**

3 Read and write the words.

week   time   me   ~~hair~~   early   sing   curly   anything

I used to have beautiful (1) _hair_ .
It was blond and (2) _____ .
Now I dye it black each (3) _____
Because it went gray so (4) _____ !

I used to wear glasses all the (5) _____ .
I couldn't see (6) _____ .
The doctor fixed my eyes for (7) _____ –
It made me want to (8) _____ !

4 🎵 CD 2 36 Listen and check. Say the poem.

1 **Read and write the words.**

| wear | help | ~~arrive~~ | do | learn |

When I was a schoolboy, …

1   … I had to _arrive_ at school before seven o'clock.

2   … I had to _____ a uniform.

3   … I had to _____ French, German, and Spanish.

4   … I had to _____ homework for two hours every night.

5   … I had to _____ the teacher with the younger students.

2 **Write sentences.**

When I lived at home, I had to work hard every day.

1   _I had to clean up._

2   _____

3   _____

4   _____

5   _____

6   _____

Now I live in my own house, I don't have to do things every day!

1 **Remember the story. Complete the sentences.**

1 The Mysterious H stole from _jewelers_ in London.

2 He stole from museums all over the _____ .

3 The story of The Mysterious H was in all the _____ .

4 He even stole the top of the Eiffel _____ .

5 He always used to leave a _____ with an *H* on it.

6 The _____ in the restaurant was wearing a ring with an *H* on it.

2 **Remember The Mysterious H's rhyme. Write the words in order.**

but / find / anywhere / here / you / look / look / there / ~~you~~ / you / can't / me

You _____ _____ _____ . _____ _____ _____ .

_____ _____ _____ _____ _____ .

3 **Where did The Mysterious H steal these things from?**
Draw lines and write sentences.

a museum
the castle
a jewelry store
an art gallery
Paris

1 _He stole the painting from an art gallery._

2 _____

3 _____

4 _____

5 _____

1 CD2 41 **Listen and write the missing words. Then say with a friend.**

1

Abby: You're famous.

Chris: I'm sorry, what did you say?

Abby: You're famous. Look.

_____ _____

_____ _____

_____ .

Chris: Oh, no! I have to change my hair again.

2

Jeremy: Oh, no! It got away!

Lionel: Again? You're just not lucky today!

Jeremy: _____ _____

_____ _____ .

Lionel: Maybe next time.

2 **Look, read, and number the sentences.**

1 **2** **3** **4**

a [ ] They were walking through **N**o**r**th **P**a**r**k when a terrible s**t**o**r**m s**t**a**r**ted.

b [1] **M**a**r**k and **Gl**o**r**ia went out at a qua**r**ter past **f**ou**r** in the m**or**ning.

c [ ] The rescue team saw the light and took **M**a**r**k and **Gl**o**r**ia to their **car**.

d [ ] They couldn't find their **car** in the **d**a**r**k, so **Gl**o**r**ia used her flashlight.

3 CD2 42 **Listen, say, and check your answers.**

1 (Values) **What can we learn from the story? Color the words.**

(Find)   (Don't)   (make)   (take)   (her)

(other people's)   (things)   (words)   (.)

2 **Look and write the words.**

> my enemy   a seed   a piece of apple
> a shoulder   a farmer   a juicy orange

1 _a piece of apple_

2 _____

3 _____

4 _____

5 _____

6 _____

3 (Think!) **Put the story in order.**

[ ] The police officer tells the farmer that Yatin is sorry.

[1] Yatin eats an orange from the tree.

[ ] Yatin goes home.

[ ] Yatin thinks about his mom and dad.

[ ] The farmer catches Yatin.

[ ] The farmer gives Yatin a bag of seeds.

[ ] The farmer goes to get the police officer.

[ ] Yatin works for the farmer.

1 **Look at the pictures. Write the story.**

One day a boy was in a store.

1 **Correct the sentences.**

1 Agatha Christie is only popular in the U.K.

No, she's popular all over the world.

2 She disappeared in the 1930s for 20 days.

_____

3 Conan Doyle was 81 when he died.

_____

4 He also wrote love stories.

_____

5 Miss Marple appeared in 11 novels.

_____

6 Sherlock Holmes' friend was named Mr. Watson.

_____

7 Sherlock Holmes used to play the piano.

_____

8 Hercule Poirot was from France.

_____

2 **Read and write the name from Activity 1.**

A 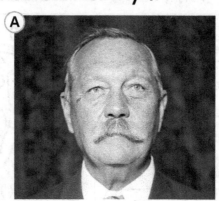   B

_____ has light hair, but he doesn't have a lot of hair. It's straight. He has a light mustache.

3 **Write a description of picture B.**

_____

_____

_____

4 **Write A and B.**

Picture _____ is a detective from a book. Picture _____ is a real writer.

1 **Remember the story. Number the pictures.**

a

b [1]

c

d

e

2 **Write two cases for Sherlock Holmes. Use ideas from the box or your own ideas.**

> in a castle   on a farm   in a big city   on a boat
> a young woman   an old man   a doctor
> a missing dog   a missing bracelet   a missing child   a missing painting
> a book in code   an old newspaper   a mysterious letter

1 The story takes place _____ .

Sherlock Holmes helps _____ find _____ .

He has to read _____ to solve the case.

2 The story takes place _____ .

Holmes and Watson _____

_____

_____

_____

1 **Match the questions with the answers.**

1 Where do you like to read?

2 How many books do you read a week?

3 What are your favorite kinds of books?

4 Do you like love stories?

5 What kinds of things do you read?

6 What's best, watching TV or reading?

a ☐ Reading, definitely, but I like TV.

b ☐ I love crime stories.

c ☐ 1 ☐ The best place is in bed!

d ☐ About two.

e ☐ No, I don't. I never read them.

f ☐ I read comic books, and I sometimes read my dad's newspaper.

2 **Look at Activity 1. <u>Underline</u> the mistakes. Then write the correct sentences.**

Lucy <u>likes reading, but she loves</u> watching TV, too. Her favorite place to read is on the couch. She reads more than three books a week. Her favorite kinds of books are science-fiction stories. She never reads historical novels. As well as reading books, she reads comic books and magazines.

Lucy loves reading, but she likes watching TV, too.

3 **Write about your reading habits.**

I like reading in bed.

1 Write the words in four groups.

~~beard~~ ~~blond~~ ~~curly~~ dark ~~farmer~~ light
mustache orange scar seed short straight

1
beard
_____
_____

2
blond
_____
_____

3
curly
_____
_____

4
farmer
_____

2 Look at Activity 1. Number the topics to match the groups.

☐ Hair color ☐ Face ☐ Story words ☐ Hair style

3 Look and draw lines to make sentences.

1 Mom's family

used to	living	in France	in the 1980s.
used	lived	by France	at the 1980s.
use to	live	on France	on the 1980s.

2 I

had to	cleaning	my bedroom	yesterday.
have to	cleaned	the kitchen	tomorrow.
has to	clean	the living room	now.

3 My mom

used	being	an actress	when she was born.
was	be	a teacher	before I was born.
used to	been	a doctor	before she was born.

4 My dad

had	help	my dad	in the store.
had to	helped	his dad	at the movies.
have to	helping	our dad	at the zoo.

6 Mythical beasts

1 Look and complete the words.

1 h o r n

2 _ o _ g _ _ _

3 _ _ c _ _

4 _ _ a t _ _ _ _ s

5 _ _ _ _ g

6 _ _ c _

7 t _ _ _ _ _

8 _ _ a _ _ s

2 Look, read, and number the texts.

a ☐ This dragon has wings. The feathers on the wings are beautiful. They have gray and white patterns. The dragon's neck is long and it has scales. There are also scales on its back, and there are feathers on its back, too. It has a short tail, a long tongue, and two horns.

b ☐ This dragon has wings. The gray feathers on the wings are beautiful. The dragon has scales on its back and also on its long neck.
It has a long tongue, a horn, and a short tail.

c ☐ This dragon has wings. The feathers on the wings are beautiful, and you can see black and white patterns on them. It has a long neck, a short tail, two horns, and a long tongue. It has feathers on its back and scales on its neck.

3 Write about the other dragon from Activity 2.

_____

_____

_____

1 Read and write t (true) or f (false).

1 The world's longest snake
The python holds the world record for the longest snake. The record-breaker was 9.92 m! The python is longer than  the anaconda, but anacondas are the world's fattest snakes.

3 The world's worst singer

The "crex-crex" song of the corncrake sounds so terrible that this bird is certainly the world's worst singer.

2 More aggressive than you think
It looks friendly in cartoons, but the hippo is probably the most dangerous land animal in Africa. (Maybe the  mosquito is even more dangerous?) Hippos are very aggressive, not scared of humans, and much more dangerous than lions.

4 Crocodiles – the smallest and the heaviest
The smallest crocodile is the dwarf crocodile of West Africa, which hardly ever grows bigger than 1.5 m long. The heaviest crocodiles are saltwater crocodiles, which can grow to 7 m long and weigh over 1,000 kg!

1 Pythons are the longest snakes, but anacondas can be fatter. — t
2 The longest snake was more than 10 m.
3 Hippos are very dangerous, but they run from humans.
4 The song of the corncrake isn't very nice at all.
5 Saltwater crocodiles aren't longer than dwarf crocodiles.

2 Write sentences.

1 Anacondas / fat / snakes in the world
   Anacondas are the fattest snakes in the world.

2 Hippos / dangerous / lions

3 Corncrakes / bad / singers in the world

4 Dwarf crocodiles / small / saltwater crocodiles

Comparatives and superlatives 71

1 **Remember the song. Correct the sentences.**

1 In my dream I met the most dangerous dragon.
   In my dream I met the most beautiful dinosaur.

2 Its head was smaller than a tractor.

3 Its neck was longer than a tower.

4 Its scales were stronger than wood.

5 Its eyes were bigger than me.

6 It had the best teeth on Earth.

2 **Write adjectives to complete the sentences.**

In my dream I met (1) _the_ _most_ _dangerous_ dinosaur. (dangerous)
Its teeth were (2) _____ _____ knives. (sharp)
Its wings were (3) _____ _____ planes. (long)
It was (4) _____ _____ animal on land. (strong)
It was (5) _____ _____ runner and
(6) _____ _____ at flying. (fast / good)

3 **Imagine a dragon or a dinosaur. Draw and write about it.**

1 **Write questions for the answers. Use the words from the box.**

Pegasus   the Sphinx   a mermaid   a unicorn   the Phoenix   a centaur

1 *What does a centaur look like?*   It's half horse and half man.

2 _____   She has the head of a woman
                                          and the tail of a fish.

3 _____   It's a bird with very big wings and
                                          red and golden feathers.

4 _____   It looks like a horse, but it has wings
                                          and can fly.

5 _____   It's a white horse with a long horn
                                          in the middle of its head.

6 _____   It looks like a lion with a human head.

2 **Think!** **Read the dialog. Write 1, 2, 3, or 4.**

A: What does Cloud _____ look like?

B: I think it looks like a dog. It's driving a car.

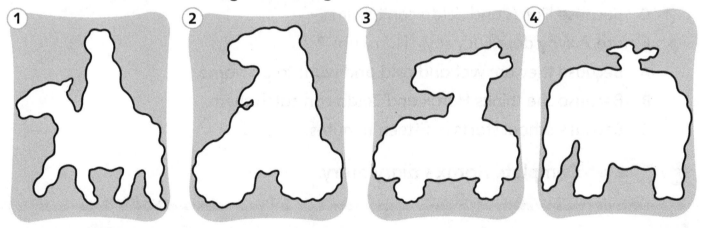

Write dialogs about the other pictures.

A: _____

B: _____

A: _____

B: _____

A: _____

B: _____

1 (Think!) **Remember the story. Put the sentences in order.**

☐ The children find a way out, but they have to jump into the pool.

1 Lucy finds a door in the dragon.

☐ Horax and Zelda see Ben and Lucy, but the children run away.

☐ On the side of the pool, they find the next line for the rhyme.

☐ The children open it and go in.

☐ It's a trap! Horax closes the door, and they can't get out.

2 (Think!) **Read and circle.**

1 Picture 1: Why is Ben standing in front of the dragon?

   A Because he hopes to see a smile on the dragon's face.

   B Because he hopes he can jump in the pool.

   C Because he hopes to see the next line on the dragon's tongue.

2 Picture 6: Why do the children jump into the pool?

   A Because it's the only way to get out.

   B Because it's a very hot day.

   C Because Horax and Zelda can't swim.

3 Picture 7: Why does Lucy say, "Hurry up!"?

   A Because they are wet and cold and want to go home.

   B Because she thinks Horax and Zelda can catch them.

   C Because school starts in fifteen minutes.

3 (Think!) **Complete Horax's diary entry.**

Today was a (1) __bad__ day for Zelda and me. We saw (2) _____ .
They were looking at (3) _____ . We were
sure the next line (4) _____ ,
but then they opened (5) _____ and
(6) _____ . Zelda and I (7) _____ .
In the end the children (8) _____ , and they
(9) _____ . Zelda and I were very (10) _____ .

1 CD3 12 **Listen and write the missing words. Then say with a friend.**

Ollie: I don't believe it. The ball's really high up in the tree.

Jem: And that tree's too dangerous to climb.

Ollie: We could get my dad's ladder.

Jem: Yes. _____ _____

_____ .

Mom: Where are you?

Dad: He's here somewhere.

Connor: Hee, hee, hee.

Mom: _____ _____

_____ _____

_____ !

Connor: Hee, hee, hee.

Mom and Dad: There you are!

Connor: Ha!

2 **Complete the chart with the words from the box.**

~~weather~~ eat team feather beans bread head meat

beast

treasure

weather

3 CD3 13 **Listen, say, and check your answers.**

1 Remember Paul's dinosaur book in the Student's Book. Read and write the words.

> a castle   vegetables   ~~a cellar~~   mice   trees

Paul has a great book about dinosaurs. He found it in
(1) _a cellar_ . The dinosaurs lived in (2) _____ . They
didn't like eating animals, so they didn't eat
(3) _____ , but they didn't eat (4) _____ either.
They loved eating (5) _____ from the garden.

2 Make sentences.

1 found / two / book / weeks / I / a / ago / unicorn / about / a
   Two weeks ago I found a book about a unicorn.

2 the / book / the / was / of / name / *Unicornia*
   _____

3 lived / forest / a fantastic / the / unicorn / in
   _____

4 lots / trees / colorful / were / of / there
   _____

5 unicorn / the / plants / eat / grass or / didn't
   _____

6 only / eat / trees / wanted to / it / purple
   _____

7 liked / book / the / I / very much / because / it / really interesting / was
   _____

3 Imagine that you found a book about a mythical beast. Write about it. Think about:

- What's the name of the book?
- Where did you find it?
- Where did the beast live?

- What did/didn't it eat?
- What did it love doing?
- Why did/didn't you like the book?

A week ago I found a book about ...

1 **Read and write *yes* or *no*.**

1 There are feathers on the dinosaur's wings.   _yes_

2 The unicorn is eating grass.   _____

3 A big, gray dragon is eating apples from a tree.   _____

4 There are some flowers below the apple tree.   _____

5 The snake with the horn is fatter than the other snake.   _____

6 There is a chicken in the bigger snake's mouth.   _____

7 There are lots of rocks in the river.   _____

8 It's sunny, but there are lots of clouds in the sky.   _____

1 Look and write the words.

snakes   seals   spiders   moths   eagles   fish   lions   ~~antelopes~~

1 antelopes

2 Write the animals from Activity 1 in two groups. Can any of the animals be in both groups?

predators	prey
	antelopes

3 Write about three of the animals.

Mice are predators. They eat moths and other insects.
Mice are also the prey of animals like cats and owls.

1 Read and write *predators* or *prey*.

All animals, (1) _predators_ and (2)_____, have to eat. Some animals eat only plants, others need plants and meat, and some eat only meat. Animals that eat meat are called (3)_____. The animals that (4)_____ eat are called (5)_____. Animals that are (6)_____ have different ways to protect themselves against their (7)_____. They use poison and weapons to fight (8)_____, their speed to run away from them, or their looks to confuse or scare the (9)_____.

2 (Values) Read the dialog. What can we learn from it? Check (✓).

Harry: Nature's horrible.

Mia: Why do you say that? Just look how beautiful everything is: those birds, the butterflies, the flowers, ...

Harry: Yes, they're beautiful, but why do some animals eat other animals? Lions eat zebras, snakes eat mice, and sharks eat smaller fish. It's terrible.

Mia: Yes, but it isn't because they're bad. They need to eat meat.

Harry: What do you mean? Can't they just eat plants?

Mia: Well, some animals eat plants only, others eat both plants and meat, and others eat meat only. They need meat to survive.

Harry: You mean they can't live without eating meat?

Mia: Exactly. Lions can't live without meat. They die.

Harry: Hmm, I think I'm beginning to understand.

Mia: Understand what?

Harry: All animals are important. Lions need meat, so they need to hunt antelopes, zebras, and other animals. When there aren't enough of them, lions can't eat.

Mia: That's right. And that's how animals die out.

- [ ] Some animals are good and some animals are bad. The bad ones are meat-eaters.
- [ ] We need to protect nature. Animals can't be allowed to die out.
- [ ] Some animals are going to die out, but it doesn't matter. Nature has enough animals.

1 **Put the dialog in order. Then listen and check.**

☐ **B:** What's strange about a white horse?

☐ **A:** In the field behind our house, 23 Park Road. It's eating all the flowers.

☐ **B:** Really? What does it look like?

1 **A:** Good afternoon. Can I speak to the director of the zoo, please?

☐ **B:** OK. Try not to scare it. I'm coming to your house right now.

☐ **A:** Well, it looks like a horse, a white horse.

☐ **B:** That's me. How can I help you?

☐ **A:** It has a horn.

☐ **B:** A white horse with a horn. Then it's a unicorn. Where did you find it?

☐ **A:** I have a strange animal. I found it this morning.

2 **Look and write a dialog. Use language from Activity 1.**

I have a strange animal. I found it this afternoon.

1 (Think!) **Which one is different in each group? Look, think, and circle.**

2 **Color the bricks to make sentences. Write in the missing words.**

1	What does	best sister _____	_____ ?
2	You're the	your sister	my mom.
3	What do	mermaids look	_____ the world!
4	That's the ugliest	is taller _____	the world!
5	My aunt	dog	_look_ like?

7 Orchestra practice

1 CD3 18 **Listen and circle.**

1 recorder / (violin)
2 trombone / trumpet
3 drums / keyboard
4 keyboard / tambourine
5 trumpet / saxophone

6 violin / harp
7 triangle / drums
8 saxophone / trombone
9 tambourine / triangle

2 **Find the triangles and write sentences.**

There's a triangle under the tambourine.

1 Read and write the words.

hers   theirs   his   yours   ~~mine~~   ours

1 Is this your bike, Ken?
Yes, it's _mine_ .

2 Is this Peter's guitar?
Yes, it's _____ .

3 This isn't my pen. Take it.
It's _____ .

4 That's a nice scooter. Is it Jane's?
Yes, it's _____ .

5 Is this where you and Lily live?
Yes, this house is _____ .

6 This is Peter and Tom's car.
Is it really _____ ?

2 Change the sentences.

1 It's my dog. It's _mine_ .
2 It's Mia's cat. It's _____ .
3 They are John and Lucy's horses. They're _____ .
4 This house is Ruby's and mine. It's _____ .
5 It's John's violin. It's _____ .
6 It's not my cap. It's your cap. It's _____ .

3 Look and write sentences.

 It's mine.

1 Remember the song. Check (✓) or put an ✗ and write sentences.

1 Sandra — silver ✗ The silver pen isn't hers.

2 Sue — silver ☐ _____

3 Tim and Nick — green ☐ _____

4 Tim and Nick — blue ☐ _____

2 Follow the lines. Answer the questions.

Olivia   Harry   Luke   Mia   George and Ella   Daisy and Jack

1 Is the cat George and Ella's?   No, it isn't theirs. It's Daisy and Jack's.
2 Is the pencil case Mia's?   _____
3 Is the book Harry's?   _____
4 Is the dog Daisy and Jack's?   _____
5 Is the pencil Olivia's?   _____
6 Is the backpack Luke's?   _____

1 Read and circle.

1 Matt is the boy **who** / **that** plays the guitar.

2 Mexico is the country **that** / **where** my cousins live.

3 The house **who** / **that** you can see over there is Bob's.

4 Claire is the girl **where** / **who** is a very good soccer player.

5 The instrument **that** / **who** George plays is the saxophone.

6 London is the city **who** / **where** I'd like to live.

2 Read and write *who*, *that*, or *where*.

1 Max is the boy ___who___ reads lots of books.

2 The instrument _____ my friend plays is the violin.

3 The town _____ my grandparents live is close to the coast.

4 Maria is the girl _____ likes listening to music.

5 The pen _____ is on the floor is Will's.

6 The farm _____ we ride horses is in the mountains.

3 Look and write four more sentences with *who* or *that*.

The boy who is reading is Jack.

The saxophone that is next to the couch is Jack's.

_____

_____

_____

_____

1 **Remember the story. Read and write the words.**

apple   hides   banana   ~~cafeteria~~   takes   cup   line   open   starts   to

Lucy and Ben go to the (1) _cafeteria_ for a drink. They order orange juice, an (2) _____ , hot chocolate, and a (3) _____ . Then Ben sees the (4) _____ on Lucy's (5) _____ . When the children are having their drinks, Horax looks in Ben's backpack, and he (6) _____ out the map. The conductor sees Horax and wants him (7) _____ leave. Horax (8) _____ the map in the trumpet. When Ben and Lucy come back, they see that Ben's backpack is (9) _____ . When the trumpet player (10) _____ , the children find the map.

2 (Think!) **Read and write _t_ (true) or _f_ (false).**

1   Pictures 1 and 2: The children know that the line is in the cafeteria.   [f]

2   Picture 4: Lucy can't read the line.   [ ]

3   Picture 5: When Horax says, "Very nice of you, kids. Thank you," he is talking to Ben and Lucy.   [ ]

4   Picture 6: When the conductor arrives, Horax thinks of a trick.   [ ]

5   Picture 7: The children know that the map is in the trumpet.   [ ]

6   Picture 8: The trick that Horax plays doesn't work.   [ ]

3 **Look and answer the questions.**

1   Is this Ben's?

No, it isn't his.

It's the conductor's.

2   Is this Lucy's?

_____

_____

3   Is this Horax's?

_____

_____

4   Is this the conductor's?

_____

_____

1 CD3 27 Listen and write the missing words. Then say with a friend.

Mom: Be careful with those plates, Tom. Maybe you should only take two at a time?

Tom: Don't worry, Mom. … Whoops!

Mom: Tom!

Tom: _____ _____

_____ , Mom.
I really am.

Deb: Where's Frank?

George: I don't know. There are just too many people.

Deb: Hey, look. There he is. Over there. Frank! Frank!

George: Oh yes, _____

_____ !

Good eye, Deb!

2 Write the words from the box in the *shirt* or the *door*.

world floor bird work short thirsty orchestra keyboard
horn curly sword her four first purple more

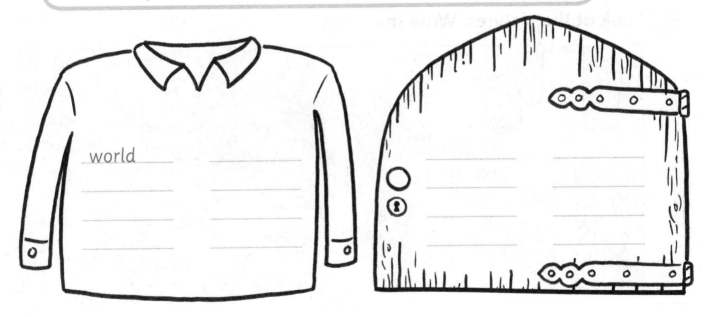

world

3 CD3 28 Listen, say, and check your answers.

1 **Values** **What can we learn from the story? Color the words.**

It's   They're   sometimes   bad

important   to   be   have

different   sad   from   his

your   friends   family   .

2 **Read and write the words.**

laughed   ~~fell off~~   silent   invite   beautiful   day

1   The bear saw a big bag that _fell off_ a car.
2   In the bag there was a _____ violin.
3   The bear played the violin all _____ .
4   One day the bear said to his friends, "I'd like to _____ you to a concert."
5   After the concert his friends were _____ .
6   The animals _____ because they didn't like his music.

3 **Look at the pictures. Write the story.**

One day the elephant saw a trumpet.

1 Read the text. Choose the correct words and write them on the lines.

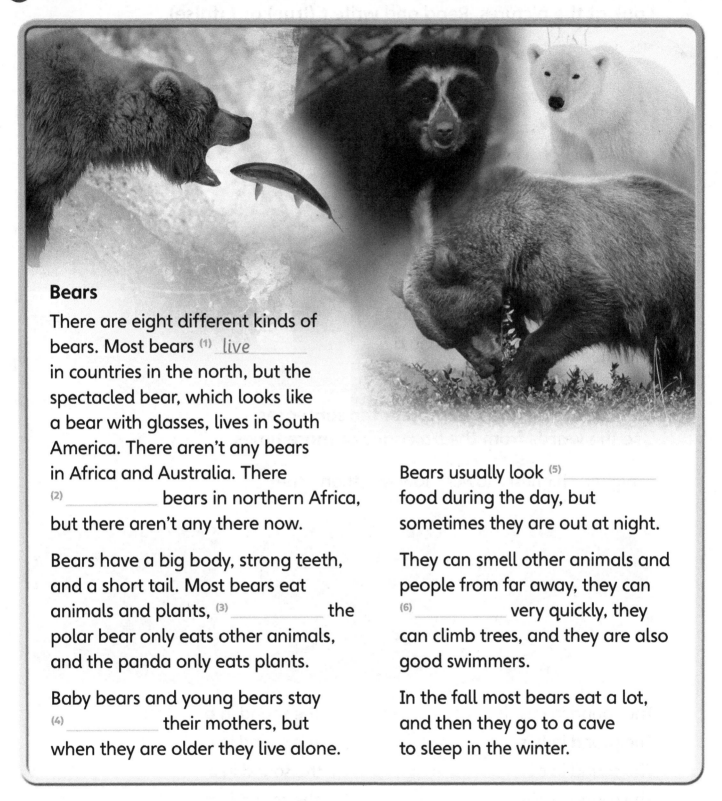

Bears

There are eight different kinds of bears. Most bears (1) _live_ in countries in the north, but the spectacled bear, which looks like a bear with glasses, lives in South America. There aren't any bears in Africa and Australia. There (2) _____ bears in northern Africa, but there aren't any there now.

Bears have a big body, strong teeth, and a short tail. Most bears eat animals and plants, (3) _____ the polar bear only eats other animals, and the panda only eats plants.

Baby bears and young bears stay (4) _____ their mothers, but when they are older they live alone.

Bears usually look (5) _____ food during the day, but sometimes they are out at night.

They can smell other animals and people from far away, they can (6) _____ very quickly, they can climb trees, and they are also good swimmers.

In the fall most bears eat a lot, and then they go to a cave to sleep in the winter.

1	living	live	lives
2	were	was	is
3	but	so	because

4	at	up	with
5	on	in	for
6	runs	run	running

1 Look at the pictures. Read and write *t* (true) or *f* (false).

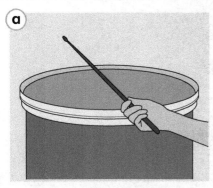 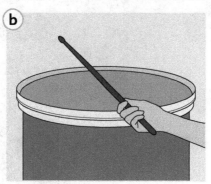 

1 The bang in **a** is louder than in **b.**   *f*

2 The bang in **b** is louder than in **c.**

3 The bang in **c** is louder than in **b.**

4 The bang in **b** is louder than in **a.**

5 The bang in **b** is the loudest.

2 Look at the pictures. Complete the sentences.
Use the words from the box once or more times.

> higher   highest   lower   lowest   than   the

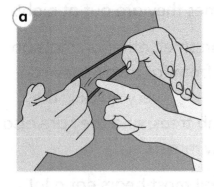 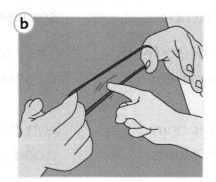 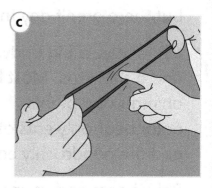

1 The sound in **a** is _lower_ _than_ the sound in **b.**

2 The sound in **b** is _____ _____ the sound in **c.**

3 The sound in **c** is _____ _____ the sound in **b.**

4 The sound in **b** is _____ _____ the sound in **a.**

5 The sound in **c** is _____ _____ .

6 The sound in **a** is _____ _____ .

1 Draw lines to match the opposites.

HIGH LOUD SHORT

LONG

QUIET LOW

2 What sound do these instruments make?
Number the pictures 1 (the lowest) to 3 (the highest).

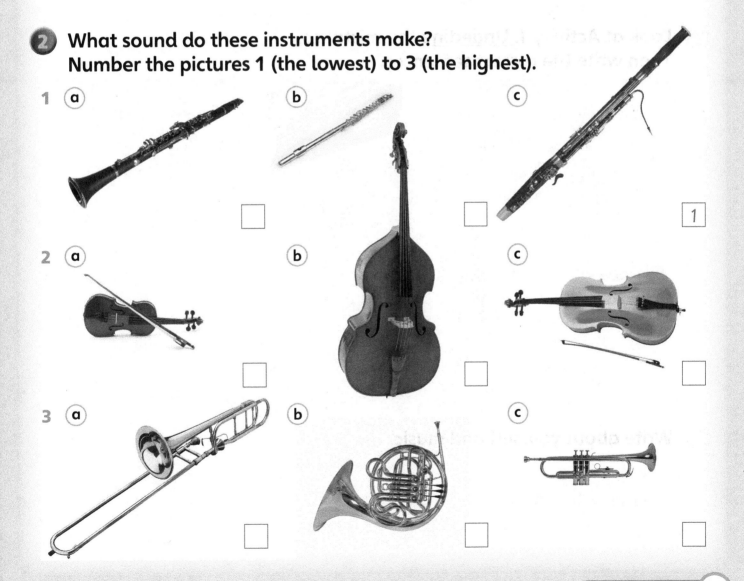

1 (a)　　　(b)　　　(c)
□　　　□　　　1

2 (a)　　　(b)　　　(c)
□　　　□　　　□

3 (a)　　　(b)　　　(c)
□　　　□　　　□

1 **Match the questions with the answers.**

1 Do you play an instrument, Lily?

2 Would you like to play an instrument?

3 Who's your favorite singer?

4 Justin Bieber? Is he from the U.S.A.?

5 And what's your favorite song?

6 Is there a song that you really don't like?

a ☐ It's Justin Bieber.

b ☐ My favorite song? It's probably "Never Say Never."

c ☐ Yes, I'd like to play the violin.

d ☐ No, not by Justin! But I really don't like "Someone Like You" by Adele.

e ☐ 1 No, I don't.

f ☐ No, he's from Canada.

2 **Look at Activity 1. Underline the mistakes. Then write the correct sentences.**

Lily plays the guitar. She wouldn't like to play the violin. Her favorite singer is Justin Bieber. He is from America. Her favorite song is "Never Say Never." There is one song that she really doesn't like. It's called "Someone Like Me." It's by Usher.

Lily doesn't play an instrument.

_____

_____

_____

3 **Write about yourself and music.**

I play the piano, and I'd like to play ...

1 **Write the words in four groups.**

drum guitar harp high low loud saxophone
tambourine triangle trombone trumpet violin

1	2	3	4
drum	guitar	high	saxophone

2 **Look at Activity 1. Number the topics to match the groups.**

☐ Stringed instruments   ☐ Sound words

☐ Wind instruments   ☐ Percussion instruments

3 **Look and draw lines to make sentences.**

1 It

isn't you	cap.	They're	my.
isn't your	caps.	He's	me.
isn't yours	book.	It's	mine.

2 The recorders

that	are on	the couch	are us.
who	are next to	the chair	are ours.
where	are under	the cabinet	are violins.

3 I

thinks	this ball	were	hers.
think	these balls	are	yours.
thinking	those balls	is	theirs.

4 The girl

who is	sitting	across from the tree	is my sister.
where is	sits	next to the tree	is hers.
that is	sit	on the tree	is my brother.

In the planetarium

1 **Read the sentences. Do the crossword puzzle. Find the secret word.**

1 This is something that you use to look at the night sky.

2 He or she flies in a rocket.

3 Earth is one of these.

4 This has a tail and it flies through the sky.

5 People stay and work here in space.

6 The night sky is full of these.

7 You use this to fly to the moon.

8 This is an alien spaceship.

9 Earth has one of these.

2 **Look at Activity 1. Number the pictures.**

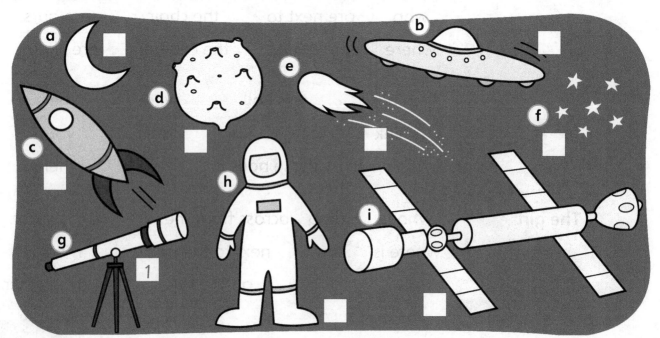

1 Follow the lines. Write the names and the sentences.

Elena : I'll be a n u r s e .

_____ : _____ t __ __ ch __ r.

_____ : _____ f __ r __ f __ ght __ r.

_____ : _____ c __ n d __ ct __ r.

_____ : _____ p __ l __ c __ __ ff __ c __ r.

2 Write five sentences about yourself.

When I grow up, I'll be an explorer.

I'll look for treasure.

I'll have lots of fun.

I'll travel the world.

I'll be very happy.

1 Remember the song. Correct the sentences.

1 The astronaut will build a space station.

   No, she'll live in a space station.

2 She'll fly to the sun in a rocket.

_____

3 She'll ride on a comet and paint its tail.

_____

4 She'll meet some aliens on the moon.

_____

5 She'll visit some of the stars.

_____

2 What will you do when you're an astronaut? Write sentences.

clean up   build   fly   ~~fix~~

1 I'll fix my rocket.   2 _____

3 _____   4 _____

3 Imagine you meet aliens on Earth. Write four sentences.

I'll show them my house.   I'll take them to the movies.

1 **Write adverbs to complete the sentences.**

1   John is a good soccer player, but yesterday he played _badly_ . (bad)

2   She sang the song _____ at the concert. (beautiful)

3   Uncle Rob is too fast on the road. He drives _____ . (dangerous)

4   When he saw the big dog, he ran back to his car _____ . (quick)

5   She loved her new toy and played _____ with it all day. (happy)

6   He didn't want to wake up his brother, so he spoke _____ . (quiet)

2 **Write sentences. Make adverbs with the adjectives from the box.**

bad   dangerous   beautiful   ~~careful~~   quiet   loud

1   He 's working carefully.

2   They _____ .

3   She _____ .

4   He _____ .

5   She _____ .

6   They _____ .

1 (Think!) **Remember the story. Put the sentences in order.**

☐ Zelda finds a poem.

☐ Lucy and Ben close the door.

☐ Ben's grandpa and a police officer arrive.

☐ 1 Lucy and Ben can't find the clue anywhere, and they go for a drink.

☐ The police officer takes Horax and Zelda away.

☐ Horax and Zelda climb inside the rocket.

2 (Values) **Read the story. What can we learn from it? Check (✓).**

"Can we have fish for dinner, please?" Gan and his younger brother Li asked their mother. "No, I'm sorry. Fish is too expensive," she answered, "but Gan, you can try to catch some in the lake."

"I'll go, too," said Li.

"No," said Gan quickly, "I'll bring enough fish for all of us."

Gan went to the lake. He saw an old man fishing, but Gan didn't speak to him. He put some bread on the hook and started fishing. After two hours, he didn't have any fish, and he decided to go home. On his way, he saw that the old man had five fish, and Gan was angry.

The next day, Li asked Gan, "Are you going fishing today?"

"There aren't any fish there," Gan answered, and he went out to play.

Li took the fishing rod and went to the lake. The old man was there again.

"Hello," said Li, "can I sit next to you?"

"Yes, of course," the old man answered.

When Li put some bread on the hook, the old man said, "The fish in this lake don't like bread, so I'll give you some corn."

After two hours, Li had five fish. "Thank you very much," he said to the old man. The old man smiled.

☐ Older people don't know anything.

☐ Older people should be friendly when they meet young people.

☐ Older people can teach us things.

1 CD4 11 **Listen and write the missing words. Then say with a friend.**

1

Carl: Look at the ball!

Millie: We did it!

Carl: Yes. _____ _____

_____ _____ .

Millie: I'll be an astronaut one day!

2

Ryan: I have no idea how to get there.

Beth: Yes, it's a little confusing, but

_____ _____ _____ .

Ryan: OK. First we need to find where we are.

Beth: Yes, and then we can see where we need to go.

2 **Look and write the words.**

farmer driver taller smaller dancer river ~~teacher~~ waiter

1 teacher   2 _____   3 _____   4 _____

5 _____   6 _____   7 _____   8 _____

3 **Listen, say, and check your answers.**

1 **Read the text and choose the best answer. Lucas is talking to an alien.**

1 **Lucas:** Can you understand me?

   Alien: A ✓ Yes, I can.

   B ☐ Yes, I am.

   C ☐ Yes, I have.

2 **Lucas:** Where is your spaceship?

   Alien: A ☐ It's great.

   B ☐ It's behind the hill.

   C ☐ Here you go.

3 **Lucas:** When did you arrive?

   Alien: A ☐ Twelve o'clock is fine.

   B ☐ In front of the house.

   C ☐ An hour ago.

4 **Lucas:** Would you like to come to my house?

   Alien: A ☐ I like your house a lot.

   B ☐ Yes, please. I'd like to see it.

   C ☐ Yes, please. My house is great.

5 **Lucas:** Are you hungry?

   Alien: A ☐ Yes, please.

   B ☐ Yes, it is.

   C ☐ Yes, I am.

6 **Alien:** Do you have any cheese?

   Lucas: A ☐ Yes, I do.

   B ☐ Yes, I like it.

   C ☐ Yes, it does.

1 Read the story. Number the pictures.

a

b

c

d

1

A hot day in the mountains

Last July my parents, my brother, and I were on vacation in the mountains.

One day when Dad was driving on a mountain road, he suddenly stopped the car. "Look!" he shouted. We all looked, but no one could see anything. "I saw an alien, I'm sure. It went over that hill."

We all got out of the car and started to walk up the hill. When we got to the top, we all saw the alien walk behind some rocks. We ran to the rocks but when we got there, it wasn't there. We walked back to the road, but now our car wasn't there. We went to the closest town and told our story to a police officer. When we finished, he told us that he had some good news. "I think we have your car," he said. He took us to the back of the police station, and there was our car. We were very happy. "And the alien?" asked Dad. "Do you believe us?"

"I think we have your alien, too. Come with me," said the police officer. We went inside, and in the police station we saw two men. One of them was wearing an alien costume. "This is your alien," said the police officer, "and this is his friend. While you were following the alien, his friend took your car."

2 Look at the pictures. Write the story.

One day we were walking ...

1 Write the names of the planets.

2 Read the text on the solar system in the Student's Book again. Complete the sentences.

1 There are __eight__ planets in our solar system.

2 The name of the biggest star in our solar system is the _____.

3 The distance through a planet or a star from one side to the other is the _____.

4 When the planets go around the sun, we say that they _____ the sun.

5 It takes Earth _____ days to orbit the sun.

6 The smaller things that orbit the planets are called _____.

3 Make sentences.

1	The sun is in	a		is different on all planets.
2	A "year" is the time it takes	b		a million times bigger than Earth.
3	The length of a year	c		a lot of moons.
4	The only star we can see	d	1	the middle of the solar system.
5	The sun is more than	e		during the day is the sun.
6	Some planets have	f		a planet to orbit the sun.

1 **Read the text. Write questions for the answers.**

Saturn is a very big planet. It's about ten times bigger than Earth, and it's about ten times farther away from the sun than Earth. The gases that make Saturn are very, very cold, so the temperature is −180°C. It's much colder than anywhere on our planet, and only Neptune is colder in our solar system. Saturn is famous for its thousands of beautiful rings, which are ice. We know a lot about Saturn because in 1979 a spacecraft, Pioneer 11, visited Saturn and took lots of pictures. Saturn has about 60 moons. This is more than any other planet.

1 _How big is Saturn?_ It's about ten times bigger than Earth.

2 _____ It's −180°C.

3 _____ No, it isn't. Neptune is the coldest planet.

4 _____ They are ice.

5 _____ It visited Saturn in 1979.

6 _____ About 60.

2 **Read, draw, and color. Write the names of the three moons.**

This is my planet. It's called Solron. It's red because it's very hot, like fire! Solron has three moons. They are called Fe, Fi, and Fo. Fo is the biggest, and Fe is the smallest. The planet also has two rings. Nobody lives on Solron because it's too hot.

1 **Put the dialog in order. Then listen and check.**

[ ] **A:** Hi, Gog. Nice to meet you. How old are you?

[ ] **B:** I'm collecting rocks. It's my hobby – intergalactic rock-collecting. What about you? Do you have a hobby?

[1] **A:** Hello. Do you speak my language?

[ ] **B:** I'm Gog.

[ ] **A:** 45 languages! That's great. I'm Mary Franklin. What's your name?

[ ] **B:** That would be great. I'd love to.

[ ] **A:** I'm 12. Gog, tell me, what are you doing here on Earth?

[ ] **B:** Yes, I do. I can understand you, Earth girl. I speak 45 languages.

[ ] **A:** Yes, I collect buttons. Would you like to see them?

[ ] **B:** I'm 235 years old. How old are you, Mary?

2 **Look and write a dialog. Use language from Activity 1.**

name?   age?

hobby?   languages?

Hello, Earth boy.

_____

_____

_____

_____

_____

_____

_____

_____

8

1 **Write the words in four groups.**

> ~~astronaut~~   ~~comet~~   ~~Earth~~   Mercury   moon   ~~Neptune~~
> rocket   Saturn   space station   star   Uranus   Venus

1

astronaut
_____
_____

2

comet
_____
_____

3

Earth
_____
_____

4

Neptune
_____
_____

2 **Look at Activity 1. Number the topics to match the groups.**

☐ Colder planets   ☐ Humans in space

☐ Hotter planets   ☐ The night sky

3 **Color some of the stars to find a planet. Write the word under the puzzle.**

V   E   M   J   I   U   N
C   P   A   T   R

_____

4 **Color the bricks to make sentences. Write in the missing words and letters.**

1	He did	you be	so I couldn't hear her.
2	She spoke	the exercise	when you grow up?
3	I'll	the old	vase careful_____ .
4	What _____	very quiet_____ ,	one day.
5	Please clean	_____ famous	very bad_ly_ .

9 At the campsite

1 Draw lines to make vacation activities.

1. sail
2. row
3. put up
4. collect
5. make
6. make
7. swing on
8. dive into
9. dry

a. the water
b. wood
c. a boat
d. a rope
e. a boat
f. a fire
g. your clothes
h. a raft
i. a tent

2 Look and write sentences.

Jamie

Freya

Paul

1 He's sailing a boat. 2 _____ 3 _____

Rebecca

Marco

Ruth

4 _____ 5 _____ 6 _____

Liam

Sophie

Matt

7 _____ 8 _____ 9 _____

1 **Look and complete the phrases.**

1 _some_ chips

2 _a bag of_ chips

3 _____ milk

4 _____ milk

5 _____ tomatoes

6 _____ tomatoes

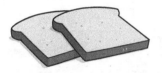

7 _____ bread

8 _____ bread

2 **Look and complete the dialogs.**

1 **A:** Would you like _a bag of candy_ ?
   B: Yes, please.

2 **A:** Let's take a _____
      to the party.
   B: That's a good idea.

3 **A:** Would you like _____
      on your pasta?
   B: No, thanks.

4 **A:** Can I have a _____ ,
      please?
   B: Yes, of course. Carrot cake or lemon cake?

5 **A:** I'd like two _____ ,
      please.
   B: That's $1.90.

1 Remember the song. Number the food.

- [ ] a bottle of juice
- [ ] a bag of chips
- [ ] a candy bar
- [ ] a loaf of bread
- [1] a piece of cheese

2 What's missing? Write sentences.

1   *The piece of cheese is missing.*   2   _____

3   _____   4   _____

3 Think! What's the problem? Read and draw lines.

We're going on a picnic with our picnic basket.

| My little sister put | a can of fruit, | some ice cream | and some eggs | in our picnic basket ... |

but ...

so we didn't eat them!

1 Write *much* or *many*, *is* or *are*.

1 How __much__ cheese __is__ there?

2 How _____ eggs _____ there?

3 How _____ apples _____ there?

4 How _____ milk _____ there?

5 How _____ bread _____ there?

6 How _____ bottles of water _____ there?

2 Look at the picture. Answer the questions from Activity 1.

1 There are three pieces

   of cheese.

2 _____

   _____

3 _____

   _____

4 _____

   _____

5 _____

   _____

6 _____

   _____

3 What else is in the fridge? Write dialogs.

A: How many candy bars are there ?

B: There are four candy bars.

A: _____ ?

B: _____

A: _____ ?

B: _____

A: _____ ?

B: _____

1 **Remember the story. Make sentences.**

1 The children find the last line   a [   ] in order.
2 Then they put the rhyme   b [   ] behind a picture.
3 They go to the lighthouse   c [   ] in a newspaper.
4 The key that they need is   d [   ] under the floor.
5 Buster helps find the chest   e [   ] on the beach.
6 Horax and Zelda read about it   f [1] on an oar.

2 **Complete Ben and Lucy's story. Use two words from the box in each sentence.**

> dragon ring conductor accident restaurant rocket door map car
> train treasure ~~shield~~ trumpet lighthouse trap man ~~knight~~ tunnel

① Lucy and Ben find the first line _on the knight's shield_____ .

② Horax tries to steal _____ .

③ Grandpa helps a man who has _____ .

④ When _____ , Ben takes the bad guys' tickets.

⑤ Grandpa wanted to catch a _____ who had _____ with *H* on it.

⑥ Horax and Zelda _____ the children _____ .

⑦ When Horax sees _____ , he puts the map _____ .

⑧ Ben and Lucy play a trick and close _____ .

⑨ They find _____ .

3 **Write the lines of the rhyme in order.**

> There's the key to end this game.

> Climb more stairs and look out west.

> In the lighthouse you will see

> Behind the picture in the frame

> Lots of stairs. Climb thirty-three!

> Look down and find the treasure chest.

In the lighthouse you will see

_____

_____

_____

_____

_____

1 CD 4 26 **Listen and write the missing words. Then say with a friend.**

1

Mom: So, Esme, what do you think?

Esme: Well, um, _____

_____ perfectly.

Mom: Yes, I know. But is it nice?
Come on, tell me.

Esme: Um, it's horrible, Mom.

2

Kate: OK, so where are we?

Chris: I'm not sure. But I think we're
really close now.

Kate: But _____ _____
do we have to go?

Chris: Um, I don't know.

2 **Look and write the words once or more times.**

bottle   can   loaf   bag   piece   cup

1 a _cup_ of **tea**

2 a _____ of **chips**

3 a _____ of **bread**

4 a _____ of **cake**

5 a _____ of **lemonade**

6 a _____ of **candy**

7 a _____ of **peas**

8 a _____ of **candy**

9 a _____ of **water**

3 CD 4 27 **Listen, say, and check your answers.**

1 (Values) **What can we learn from the story? Color the words.**

(Don't)   (Do)   (tell)   (do)

(bad)   (happy)   (stories)   (things)   (to)

(from)   (animals)   (ocean)   (.)

2 **Look at the pictures and the letters in the box. Write the words.**

(~~ctiks~~ renas shomromu thosg)

1 _____   2 _____   3 _____   4 stick

3 **Look at the pictures. Write the story.**

One day Rosy went into the forest.

1 CD4 29 Listen and draw lines.

Jane   Vicky   Paul   Fred

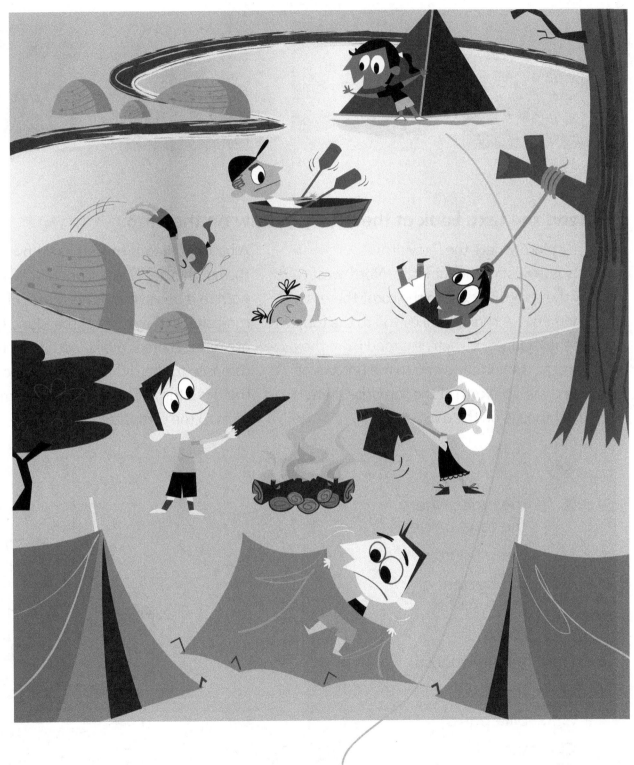

Jack   Daisy   Sally

1 **Look and write the words.**

a chair lift   cliffs   a bike path   ~~a ferry~~

1   a ferry   2 _____   3 _____   4 _____

2 **Read the text. Look at the key and draw on the map.**

The place where the ferry arrives is southwest of the campsite. Northwest of the campsite close to the coast there is a mountain. A chair lift takes you to the top of the mountain. There is a road from the ferry to the campsite and to the bottom of the chair lift. North of the campsite there is a lighthouse on the coast.

A bike path leads from the campsite to the lighthouse. There is another bike path to a beach that is northeast of the campsite. In the south of the island there are cliffs. There is a bike path from the campsite to the cliffs. In the southeast there is a farm. There is a road from the farm to the campsite.

Key

X   the place where the ferry arrives

M   the mountain

O   the bottom of the chair lift

- - - - roads

L   the lighthouse

F   the farm

. . . . bike paths

CCC   the cliffs

1 Look at Mia's map. Read, draw, measure, and answer.

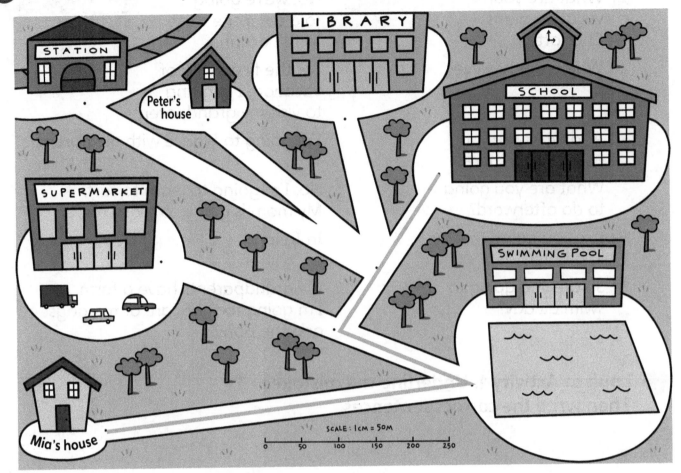

What's the distance by road from:

1 … Mia's house to her school?   about _950_ meters

2 … Mia's house to the station?   about _____ meters

3 … Mia's house to the supermarket?   about _____ meters

4 … the swimming pool to the station?   about _____ meters

5 … the supermarket to the library?   about _____ meters

2 Read and write *t* (true) or *f* (false).

1 Mia's house is about 800 m from Peter's house.   `f`

2 Peter's house is about 600 m from the swimming pool.   ☐

3 Mia has to walk farther to school than Peter.   ☐

4 The library is farther from the school than it is from the swimming pool.   ☐

5 The station is closer to the supermarket than it is to the library.   ☐

1 Match the questions with the answers.

1 What are your vacation plans, Charlotte?

a ☐ No, we're going to a campsite close to the ocean.

2 Where do they live?

b [1] For the first week of vacation, I'm going to visit my grandparents.

3 And what are you going to do there?

c ☐ I'm going to France with my parents.

4 What are you going to do afterward?

d ☐ No, I'm going to learn to surf. My mom is going to teach me.

5 Are you going to stay in a hotel?

e ☐ In Ireland.

6 So are you going to swim all day?

f ☐ My grandparents have a farm, and I'm going to take care of the dogs and the pony.

2 Look at Activity 1. Underline the mistakes. Then write the correct sentences.

Charlotte is going to visit her <u>uncle and aunt</u>. They have a hotel in Spain. There she is going to take care of the cows. Then she is going to France with her brother. There she is going to build sandcastles all day. In France Charlotte is going to stay at a hotel.

Charlotte is going to visit her grandparents.

_____

_____

_____

_____

3 Write about your vacation plans.

This summer I'm going ...

1 Think! **Which one is different in each group? Look, think, and circle.**

1

2

3

2 **Look and draw lines to make sentences.**

1 How		little	bread	do we	need?
		much	eggs	are we	needs?
		many	egg	are there	needing?

2 Would		he	like	a bag of	water?
		she	likes	a bottle of	chips?
		you	liked	a can of	tomatoes?

3 How		many	milk	are there	on the table?
		much	cheese	is there	next to the chair?
		old	books	there is	in the fridge?

4 Can I		has	a can	about	lemonade, please?
		had	a bag	in	milk, please?
		have	a glass of	of	chips, please?

What did you like best?

1 In the museum

Color your favorite lessons.

- singing the song
- acting out our Egyptian cat play
- reading The Explorers story
- reading *The secret of the Egyptian cat*
- writing an ad
- learning about museums

Word focus Write three new words.

_____ _____ _____

Grammar focus Write two sentences about yourself.

_____

_____

Now tell a friend what you liked and didn't like in Unit 1.

2 The world around us

Color your favorite lessons.

- singing the song
- finding out about our free time
- reading The Explorers story
- learning about life in art
- writing about my favorite outdoor place

Word focus Write three new words.

_____ _____ _____

Grammar focus Write two sentences about yourself.

_____

_____

Now tell a friend what you liked and didn't like in Unit 2.

3 Danger!

Color your favorite lessons.

- singing the song
- acting out our emergency services play
- reading The Explorers story
- reading *The day the ocean went out*
- writing a story about an accident
- learning about fire safety

Word focus Write three new words.

_____ _____ _____

Grammar focus Write two sentences about yourself.

_____

_____

Now tell a friend what you liked and didn't like in Unit 3.

④ Two round-trip tickets

Color your favorite lessons.

- singing the song
- reading The Explorers story
- acting out our ticket office play
- learning about forces
- writing a notice for a school bulletin board

Word focus — Write three new words.

_____ _____ _____

Grammar focus — Write two sentences about yourself.

Now tell a friend what you liked and didn't like in Unit 4.

⑤ Police!

Color your favorite lessons.

- singing the song
- reading The Explorers story
- reading *Yatin and the orange tree*
- learning about crime fiction
- finding out about our reading habits
- writing a book review

Word focus — Write three new words.

_____ _____ _____

Grammar focus — Write two sentences about yourself.

Now tell a friend what you liked and didn't like in Unit 5.

⑥ Mythical beasts

Color your favorite lessons.

- singing the song
- reading The Explorers story
- learning about predators and prey
- acting out our unusual animal play
- drawing and writing about an imaginary beast

Word focus — Write three new words.

_____ _____ _____

Grammar focus — Write two sentences about yourself.

Now tell a friend what you liked and didn't like in Unit 6.

7 Orchestra practice

Color your favorite lessons.

singing the song

finding out about music in our class

reading The Explorers story

reading The bear's dream

writing about my favorite band or singer

learning about how we make sounds

Word focus — Write three new words.

_____ _____ _____

Grammar focus — Write two sentences about yourself.

_____

_____

Now tell a friend what you liked and didn't like in Unit 7.

8 In the planetarium

Color your favorite lessons.

singing the song

acting out our interview with an alien

reading The Explorers story

learning about the solar system

writing a space diary entry

Word focus — Write three new words.

_____ _____ _____

Grammar focus — Write two sentences about yourself.

_____

_____

Now tell a friend what you liked and didn't like in Unit 8.

9 At the campsite

Color your favorite lessons.

singing the song

finding out about our vacation plans

reading The Explorers story

reading The snares in the forest

writing a vacation leaflet

learning about map reading

Word focus — Write three new words.

_____ _____ _____

Grammar focus — Write two sentences about yourself.

_____

_____

Now tell a friend what you liked and didn't like in Unit 9.